Messy Social Work

of related interest

Social Work, Cats and Rocket Science
Stories of Making a Difference in Social Work with Adults
Elaine James, Rob Mitchell and Hannah Morgan,
with Mark Harvey and Ian Burgess
Forewords by Lyn Romeo and Mark Neary
ISBN 978 1 78592 519 1
eISBN 978 1 78450 985 9

How to Survive in Social Work
Neil Thompson and John McGowan
ISBN 978 1 83997 807 4
eISBN 978 1 83997 808 1

Social Work Under Pressure
How to Overcome Stress, Fatigue and Burnout in the Workplace
Kate van Heugten
ISBN 978 1 84905 116 3
eISBN 978 0 85700 223 5

Motivational Interviewing for Working with Children and Families
A Practical Guide for Early Intervention and Child Protection
Donald Forrester, David Wilkins and Charlotte Whittaker
ISBN 978 1 78775 408 9
eISBN 978 1 78775 409 6

Making Connections with Vulnerable Children & Families
Creative Tools & Resources for Practice
Jan Horwath
Illustrated by Stevie Wilkinson, Graphics by Andy Wilkinson
ISBN 978 1 78775 794 3
eISBN 978 1 78775 795 0

The Social Work, Cats and Rocket Science Guide to Rights-Based Practice
An A–Z, from Advocacy to Zones of Influence
Edited by Elaine James and Rob Mitchell
Forewords by Sara Ryan and School of Rock and Media
ISBN 978 1 80501 231 3
eISBN 978 1 80501 232 0

MESSY SOCIAL WORK

Learning from Frontline Practice with Children and Families

Richard Devine

Foreword by Professor Andrew Turnell

Jessica Kingsley Publishers
London and Philadelphia

First published in Great Britain in 2025 by Jessica Kingsley Publishers
An imprint of John Murray Press

2

Copyright © Richard Devine 2025
Foreword copyright © Andrew Turnell 2025

The right of Richard Devine to be identified as the Author of the Work has been
asserted by him in accordance with the Copyright, Designs and Patents Act 1988.

All rights reserved. No part of this publication may be reproduced, stored
in a retrieval system, or transmitted, in any form or by any means without
the prior written permission of the publisher, nor be otherwise circulated
in any form of binding or cover other than that in which it is published and
without a similar condition being imposed on the subsequent purchaser.

A CIP catalogue record for this title is available from the
British Library and the Library of Congress

ISBN 978 1 80501 006 7
eISBN 978 1 80501 007 4

Printed and bound in the United States by Integrated Books International

Jessica Kingsley Publishers' policy is to use papers that are natural,
renewable and recyclable products and made from wood grown in
sustainable forests. The logging and manufacturing processes are expected
to conform to the environmental regulations of the country of origin.

Jessica Kingsley Publishers
Carmelite House
50 Victoria Embankment
London EC4Y 0DZ

www.jkp.com

John Murray Press
Part of Hodder & Stoughton Ltd
An Hachette Company

The authorised representative in the EEA is Hachette Ireland,
8 Castlecourt Centre, Dublin 15, D15 XTP3, Ireland (email: info@hbgi.ie)

Contents

Acknowledgements. 7

Foreword 9
PROFESSOR ANDREW TURNELL AM

Preface 13

1. Deciding to Be a Social Worker 17

2. Working with Children 31

3. Working Directly with Children. 49

4. Working with Parents. 67

5. Working Directly with Parents. 81

6. Assessment: Making Meaning and Links 99

7. Helping Children and Families. 129

8. Making Decisions and Removing Children 145

9. Managing Time and Making a Difference 161

10. The Child Protection Social Worker Role 171

References 183

Index 187

Acknowledgements

I T DOESN'T SEEM RIGHT TO HAVE JUST MY NAME on the front of this book. Since my journey into social work as a student, I have benefited from many social work practitioners, including lecturers, practice educators and all my managers. I, and this book, would not be here without them. I have also been fortunate to have consistently worked with dedicated, skilled and compassionate colleagues. Some have taught me wisdom; some have taught me how to write an assessment or make a phone call; some have taught me how to interact with a child; and some have made me laugh at exactly the right time about the absurdities and challenges of the social work role.

This book relies heavily on my experiences with children and families. However, every precaution has been taken to respect their privacy through the anonymization process (**the cases written about are composites, and all names and details have been changed**). Nonetheless, the lessons I have learned, detailed in this book, are real and, as you will see, numerous. I am indebted to each and every child, parent and family member, for they have taught me far more than I could teach them. This is yet another way in which the social worker, parent–child relationship is unequal. I can't change that, but my biggest hope is that I have shown them the dignity, respect and humanity they deserve in this book.

Particular mention goes to the wonderful and kind practitioners who have read some or all of this book. They have given up their time to offer constructive, insightful reflections, and I couldn't be more grateful. Thank you, Rebecca Carr-Hopkins, Eleanor Chatburn,

Fabienne dos Santos Sousa, Robbie Duschinsky, Donald Forrester, Melody Lewis, Julia Mannes, Eileen Munro, Pamela Parker and Samantha Phippard. I am especially thankful to Jenny Gibbs, Tessa Godfrey, Laura Mucha, Dihini Pilimatalawwe and Andrew Turnell. In writing this book, my friend and colleague, Andy Black, has been an enormous source of support and help, essentially coaching me throughout the time I was writing. I am very grateful for his encouragement, incisive feedback and clarifying oversight.

Thank you to Stephen Jones and the Jessica Kingsley Publishers team, who allowed me to turn a dream into a reality. Stephen's diligent feedback and suggestions significantly improved the manuscript.

Finally, I wanted to thank my family. My daughter and son have filled my life with more joy and love than I knew was possible. My wife, Rebecca, has been incredibly supportive, and without her unwavering love, kindness and sense of humour, this book wouldn't have been possible. I dedicate this book to them.

Foreword

PROFESSOR ANDREW TURNELL AM

THIS BOOK IS EXCEPTIONAL AND ALMOST COMPLETELY UNIQUE! That may sound like overblown hyperbole, but it is simply an assertion of fact.

Any review of social work literature reveals that its most overlooked voice is that of the practitioner. Professor Ann Weick (2000, p.396), in a beautiful short paper titled 'Hidden voices', states 'social work has been unable to give voice to its work...a chasm of silence' surrounds what social workers do and experience on a daily basis.

The 'chasm of silence' described by Weick reflects the 'theory–practice' gap that bedevils social work. A colleague of mine is fond of the phrase that while 'practice is a bird in flight, theory is too often a dead parrot at the bottom of a cage'. As we consider this book it is important to reflect a little on why this is so.

Much could be said about the disconnect of theory with practice, but I would suggest a significant part of the problem lies in the fact that those who write often have limited experience in practice, and practitioners rarely write for the record. Probably the biggest challenge any practitioner faces is how to describe their practice and decision-making that they know is not neat and tidy and they can never be certain they did enough or that they got it right. Canadian Gerald de Montigny (a social work practitioner, author of the only other child protection book that I am aware of) writes that he knew his practice 'did not conform to the idealizations of the texts and the high aspirations of the academy' (de Montigny 1995, p.109).

So, not only is Rich's[1] book unique, Rich (although he absolutely would not claim it for himself) is a unique social worker. He has taken the time to reflect deeply, read widely, and then talk and write openly about his work and how he makes sense of it. Since practice is never perfect or neat, it is, as Rich's title reflects, an articulation of 'Messy Social Work'.

I want to record here a heartfelt thank you to Rich, for mustering the courage and vulnerability required to write this work. Where Rich found the time to write this book while also continuing his work in the field I have no idea. It's further evidence of his uniqueness.

There has been a lot written over the years about the 'reflexive' social worker. The majority is written by academics often critical of practice and decision-making they review before going on to say what they believe reflexivity is. What Rich has eloquently described in this book is what real, enacted social work reflexivity actually is. As such this book should be required reading for all social workers, to keep us grounded in the 'smell of practice' (to use Harry Ferguson's brilliant phrase; Ferguson 2011, p.17).

I now want to offer some comments about the content of the book.

The first chapter tells the story of Rich's life and how he came to be a social worker. Perversely, a profession all about the personal tends always to avoid talking personally about our own biographies. This is problematic because how we do our work is always shaped by who we are and what brought us to the profession. By anchoring this book in his own story, Rich gives us a further demonstration of professional reflexivity.

Rich then moves on to cover working with children and parents. Social work in general and child protection practice in particular always takes you to your next level of incompetence. Rich poignantly

---

[1] I use 'Rich' to refer to my colleague Richard Devine in this Foreword since that is how he wants to be addressed.

conveys the complexities, uncertainties and challenges of working with children and parents. He speaks directly and does not mince words when he talks about the difficulties of the work: 'the role of a child protection social worker is inherently conflict-ridden. The main reason for conflict is that we often work with parents who don't want to work with us'. This understanding has to be front and centre, since most social work training tends to focus on working with voluntary clients. What makes this book compelling is that, alongside the challenges, Rich provides his ideas about how to go about this work, anchored always in examples from his own practice.

Subsequent chapters unpack assessment and decision-making, including the elephant in the child protection room – exploration of removing and reunifying children. Grounded again in his experience, Rich eloquently describes the cognitive aspects of the work while also detailing the heartbreaks and the emotional intelligence required to do this work well.

Rich's discussion of time management for practitioners is invaluable given the increasing pressures social workers face. I particularly like the fact that Rich emphasizes its importance while also being clear that time management skills are not a panacea to the myriad challenges of the social work role.

In committing himself to the sustained work required to prepare and bring this book to publication, Rich has made an invaluable contribution to the social work profession. I draw again on de Montigny, who wrote 'we need (to articulate) practice that celebrates the equivocal, the confusing, the chaos and the mystery of the everyday' (1995, p.221). This is exactly what Rich has achieved in this work, and I thank him for it.

Preface

IN THE PAGES THAT FOLLOW, you will not find the glossy veneer of idealized social work, nor will you encounter neatly packaged success stories with celebratory endings. Instead, what you hold in your hand is an exploration of my journey as a child protection social worker – a journey marked by complexity and a profound struggle to navigate the murky waters of human suffering and societal inadequacies.

The social work *I wanted* to write is sanitized and has clean edges and triumphant outcomes. The social work *I read* about often fails to capture the nuances of the daily challenges faced by practitioners, overlooking the complexities inherent in our efforts to bring about change. In my opinion, social work practice is often criticized in bad faith by those who fail to acknowledge the context shaping it. Or, in an attempt to counteract this, the realities of practice are over-simplified and presented in a more appealing but less accurate light.

However, the social work *I experienced* was messy, and whether I was making a positive difference wasn't at all obvious to me. And yet, amidst the uncertainty and chaos, there were moments of clarity – and moments when, seemingly against the odds, I established a connection – relationally, to a child or parent, metaphorically, to the purpose of the work, and spiritually, to myself and life itself.

My intention with this book is to offer an authentic portrayal of the highs and lows, the triumphs and tribulations, that define the landscape of child protection social work. And along the way, I share with you what I have learned in the hope that you:

- Can recognize aspects of yourself in this book
- Avoid some of the mistakes I made
- Find ideas that help you help children and families.

This book is neither a manual nor a textbook. And it is not a manifesto. Instead, it is a first-person account, and through that lens, I explore some of the defining features of child protection social work practice. For that reason, it is quite unlike any other social work book. I draw heavily on theory and research, but if I have managed it successfully, this doesn't take centre stage.

Nowhere is this more evident than in the first chapter, looking at my childhood – arguably where all social workers begin their journey into the profession. No one's childhood is the same, and the links between someone's upbringing and their decision to become a social worker might not be as clearly linked as I experienced them to be. But look back at the life of any social worker, and experiences and events will be found that steered them in the direction of this work.

After exploring my upbringing, which I do as a way of introducing myself, sharing how I became a social worker and examining how past experiences can influence our practice, for better or worse, I explore the key areas of child protection practice – areas like direct work with children and parents, assessment and offering support – areas that I think constitute the bread and butter of social work. Finally, I end the book by reflecting on the role of a child protection social worker and returning to some of the themes of the first chapter.

As you turn the pages that follow, I hope that you will find not only an honest account of the challenges inherent in child protection social work, but also the opportunities for growth, connection and, ultimately, transformation.

Before you get started, it is important to recognize at this point that there are several limitations to writing the book in the way I have. I won't outline them all here, except for one, which I think is critical to acknowledge. I am a white male in a profession predominantly occupied by women, and having worked primarily in areas with a white British population, I recognize that my experiences will not fully capture the diversity of social workers and families in this field. It is crucial to acknowledge that race, ethnicity, gender and other intersecting identities shape both the experiences of social workers and the dynamics of the communities they serve.

As such, my perspective may not reflect the challenges faced by social workers from marginalized backgrounds or the unique needs of families from diverse cultural and ethnic backgrounds. Taking account of the privileges afforded to me by identities and experiences, I encourage readers to approach the book with a critical lens and to seek out diverse perspectives to gain a more comprehensive understanding of the profession and the communities it serves.

Finally, it is my hope that, together, we can work towards a more inclusive, equitable and compassionate practice – one that honours the dignity and worth of every individual and family we serve.

CHAPTER 1

Deciding to Be a Social Worker

M ANY SOCIAL WORKERS enter the profession with experience of some of the issues in life that social workers are there to help with. They may have values or beliefs that fed into their decision to carry out this work – and I'm no exception to this. In this chapter I share some of my experiences in order to illuminate some of the reasons why I became a social worker, and how that influenced both my approach and practice.

Redemptive helping and healing

When my dad was 10 years old, police officers and social workers rushed into his home, and he 'immediately ran under the cubby hole in absolute terror'. I can picture him as a little boy, tucked away and hidden in a dark corner. Eyes wide, pulse racing and adrenaline saturating his body.

Suddenly, a hand reached in to grab hold of him. Out of fear and panic, he resorted to animalistic self-protection and bit the person. He was eventually dragged out from underneath the cubby hole by a police officer. The police officer photographed my dad and his brothers and sisters, and then placed them into care (with separate foster carers).

By this point, my dad's mum had already left to begin a new

relationship. This was the first of many forms of abandonment my dad experienced throughout his life, although I suspect it was the most profound. After my dad's mum had left, my dad, along with his brothers and sisters, were cared for by their dad, who went on to abuse one of his sisters. This was then discovered by professionals, unbeknownst to my dad, and without any warning, my dad was separated from his dad and removed from his care.

Twenty-seven schools later, living through multiple different care homes – including one where he was abused – he entered adulthood traumatized, angry, fearful, impulsive and addicted to drugs and alcohol.

My dad met my mum when they were both 17. My mum was the youngest of seven children. She was the only one of her siblings who had gone to grammar school. Despite their very different backgrounds, she fell quickly and deeply in love with my dad.

By the time my dad was the age I am writing this, he and my mum had had four children together.

My dad's adulthood was characterized by drugs and alcohol use, and included episodes in a psychiatric hospital due to drug-induced psychosis. During this time, he was violent, unpredictable and impervious to my mum's attempts to help him. My mum remained infatuated with him despite his flaws, desperately and unyieldingly clinging to his potential. She believed that deep down he was fundamentally a good person who would, and could, change.

My mum would also occasionally glimpse my dad's love for her, and the power of this would encourage her to persevere with the relationship. This took its toll, and in the process she needed to block out the emotional and psychological pain caused by his harmful behaviour, although 'her body kept the score'.[1]

By the time I was born, something had changed. My dad attended a drug and alcohol rehabilitation centre and became sober for the first time in his adult life. His violent outbursts, the legal consequences of his drug use and being sectioned due to drug-induced psychosis had

---

1   To borrow from the title of Dr Bessel van der Kolk's 2005 book on trauma.

done little to deter him previously. However, once he decided to stop using drugs, he went to a drug and alcohol rehabilitation centre that offered him a highly accepting, supportive, yet challenging support programme to help him abstain. He was supported to address, or at least reduce, some of the emotional distress tied to his childhood experiences of rejection, abandonment and instability.

My dad wrote in his diary, 'I attended the birth and held my wife's hand, and he was born, and with some sobriety he was the only child born while I wasn't actively addicted.' Several years passed. He attended university, became a social worker, and achieved the greatest level of stability and contentment in his adult life.

Unfortunately, it didn't last. My dad left his job on health grounds, finding it hard to cope with working long hours as well as my mum's deteriorating health. The years of living with my dad had compromised my mum's immune system, and she became unwell – with severe depression and chronic fatigue. To make matters worse, as soon as my dad stopped working, he began using drugs and alcohol again. He wrote in his diary, 'It was shortly after I left my job, I took one pill and within a short period of time I was a fully-fledged alkie and druggie, my son Richard saw some of the old behaviour that he had never experienced before, and I feel this contaminated him... this disgusts me.'

I was eight years old when this happened. My dad was right – I did see some of his old behaviour. My childhood felt like a story of two halves: before my dad's descent into self-sabotage, shame and addiction, my life was defined by love, stability and innocence. Despite what was to follow, the stability afforded to me during my early years – although I remember little from that time – would undoubtedly have positively impacted my development and outcomes.

My dad's relapse changed everything. The love, care and attention he had shown me up until that point slowly and increasingly withered away as he was swallowed up by the addiction that had plagued him for most of his adult life. During his relapse, my dad had left me. Where had he gone? He was still there physically, but emotionally and relationally, he was disappearing. I was devastated. I felt heartbroken for my loss, yet unable to do anything about it.

I began shutting off emotionally.

My mum began disappearing too – she slept more and sank into depression.

In adulthood, and after I qualified as a social worker, I learned about the dynamic-maturational model of attachment and adaptation (DMM) developed by American developmental psychopathologist Dr Patricia Crittenden. The DMM would become the most important and influential theoretical model, in both a personal and a professional context. With the help of this model, I learned that, without any awareness, I had found a way to deal with the increasing lack of availability my parents had for me during my childhood. I tried to rely on my parents less and block out feelings of sadness or anger, having learned that my parents were not able to deal with or respond to my feelings.

I created a rule: 'Don't express feelings'. And I tried to please and placate my mum, which led to a second rule, 'Constantly think about and anticipate my mum's needs'. These two rules combined led to the development of an unconscious strategy of (1) minimizing my own needs and (2) anticipating and meeting the needs of others (a 'compulsive caregiving strategy' in DMM terms).

This strategy worked for me in the context I grew up in, as it improved my relationship with my mum, helping me cope with the limited emotional support I received from both my parents. However, it also led to a pervasive feeling of inadequacy and worthlessness as my emotions were unintentionally yet consistently ignored or devalued by my parents. As a child, I couldn't separate the rejection of my feelings from the rejection of my fundamental self. Shame was the outcome.

At 16 years old, one week shy of my 17th birthday, my dad died. The doctors said he died of cancer; I think he died of trauma and shame. To me, psychologically at least, my dad had died a thousand times before he physically died. Every time I went to him, and he wasn't there for me, our relationship founded on stability and love suffered a blow.

I didn't cry at his funeral. My best friend came, and as I watched him wipe the tears trickling down his cheeks, I thought, 'How unusual'. I'd spent the last several years detaching myself from emotions – especially negative ones. I had become so efficient and effective that I didn't realize I was doing it.

After my dad died, I asked my mum, 'Why did dad become a social worker?' She said my dad had told her it was because he wanted to prevent what had happened to him happening to others. I immediately felt really sad that he hadn't been able to do this (because he quit and then relapsed), so I decided in that moment that I would finish what he could not.

When my dad died, I stayed on at sixth form, although I was asked to leave due to poor behaviour. With the support of a Connexions worker,[2] I attended the Prince's Trust for young people out of education, employment and training. I'd take a one-hour bus trip five days a week, listening to Skinnyman's *Council Estate of Mind* on my MP3 player.

I enjoyed the Prince's Trust programme and went on to complete a BTEC National Diploma in Health and Social Care (I was the only male among 36 females). I received an Educational Maintenance Allowance (EMA) of £30 a week, which covered my bus fare and left me with a few quid to get wasted with my friends on the weekend. Looking back, I was twin-tracking my life – pursuing my ambition to become a social worker while also drinking alcohol and taking drugs problematically.

I had started drinking and taking drugs at the same time my dad died; I instantly found great relief in taking them. In other words, I loved taking them. Or, more accurately, I loved the feeling they gave me. I had been suppressing all my negative feelings psychologically. Now, I had access to a range of substances that would do a far more effective job than I could. I didn't have to suppress or confront the unbearable feelings of rejection, loss and feelings of worthlessness or

---

2 Connexions was a UK government information, advice, guidance and support service for young people aged 13 to 19, from 2000 to 2012.

inadequacy. I could drink some alcohol or take some drugs, and all that internal psychological distress would disappear into the background.

Some of my friends used the same substances, albeit very differently. For them, it was to enhance an experience or a period of experimentation. When my friends used alcohol or drugs, they did so intermittently. I, however, used them to define my experience, and quickly became dependent on them.

Many drugs are effective because they artificially create satisfying emotional states that typically derive from being well connected to others. Or because they numb the psychological distress caused by fractured or abusive relationships. In an interview, renowned child psychiatrist and author Dr Bruce Perry said,

> A child who is stressed early in life will be more overactive and reactive. He is triggered more easily, is more anxious and distressed. Now, compare a person – child, adolescent or adult – whose baseline arousal is normal with another whose baseline state of arousal is at a higher level. Give them both alcohol: both may experience the same intoxicating effect, but the one who has this higher physiological arousal will have the added effect of feeling pleasure from the relief of that stress. It's similar to when with a parched throat you drink some cool water: the pleasure effect is much heightened by the relief of thirst. (cited in Maté 2018, pp.196–197)

Not only did my experiences cause me sadness and pain, but they also led to the development of a strategy that closed me off emotionally, especially within close relationships. This deprived me of access to genuine connections with others, even when they were available. Canadian physician and world-renowned expert in addiction, Gabor Maté, eloquently captured how experiences in childhood can have lasting effects in his bestseller, *In the Realm of Hungry Ghosts*: 'The greatest damage done by neglect, trauma or emotional loss is not the immediate pain they inflict but the long-term distortions they induce in the way a developing child will continue to interpret the world and her situation in it' (2018, p.350).

To put it in technical terms, I had limited access to the biochemical and emotional sustenance available through relationships. When I took alcohol and drugs, I knew about the negative effects and understood the risks and harms associated with the various substances. Nevertheless, it was a trade-off I was willing to make. I chose to take drugs, but I chose them in the context of unbearable psychological distress and a lack of relational support that would support the resolution of that distress. I also had a lack of hope for the future. In other words, it was the most effective, albeit short-term, solution available to me.

After two years of college, at the age of 19, I moved out of my home and the council estate I had grown up in to a university campus where I studied social work. This was a difficult transition. I was painfully shy, insecure and useless at making friends. I was nevertheless excited for fresher's week, anticipating all the fun and new friends I would make.

Instead, on the first night, I went to the student union knowing no one, unable to connect with people, and drank alcohol until I blacked out. Despite living within a few minutes of my lectures, I was often late and dressed in a way that made where I came from obvious: Nike Air Max's, worn-out joggers, a hoodie and a fake New York Yankees cap. In between lectures and during days off, I retreated to my room and passed the time smoking cannabis. Unable to find my place socially with my peers, who all seemed confident and self-assured, I missed my friends at home who spoke, looked and acted as I did. I recently emailed my university lecturer, Sarah Leigh, and she recalled, 'I remember you as the puzzled-looking "boy" wandering about Glenside looking a bit lost! (I think you were a bit lost).'

I barely passed my first year. However, as the degree continued, a few things happened. First, the degree was three years of self-development and therapy, and I learned a lot about myself and my upbringing. Second, I began to see that I had a future, and this, among other factors, led me to re-evaluate my drug use. And I quit.

Unsurprisingly, my grades improved after this. Although I no longer took drugs, some of the deep-rooted and underlying feelings that had led me to take them didn't dramatically alter, but I was able to redirect my addictive tendencies into a more socially acceptable and less harmful direction. It was channelled in the direction of my role as a child protection social worker. In 2010, at the age of 22, I qualified as a social worker and went to work in a long-term child protection team.

My motivation for being a social worker

As a student or newly qualified social worker, I was often asked why I had become one. I would say that I wanted to work with children and make a positive difference. This is only partly true, however. Another key reason was that I felt compelled to finish what my dad couldn't.

Several years after becoming a social worker, I learned what my dad was attempting to achieve. It was one of those penny-dropping moments.

I attended a social work conference where a psychotherapist explained that many of us in the helping profession often attempt to rescue our childhood selves vicariously by helping others. Suddenly, what my mum had told me about my dad's reasons for becoming a social worker several years prior had new meaning. My dad had been attempting to rescue his childhood self, he was trying to heal his childhood trauma. I realized that I was trying to rescue my dad's childhood self on his behalf.

Over time, I have come to believe that it is important to acknowledge the more self-serving reasons we do this work – otherwise, it runs the risk of interfering with our practice. For example, during supervision with my manager, we were discussing a long-term alcoholic and single father, let's call him James. James was stealing to fund his addiction and neglecting his children's needs. Despite these obvious risk factors, I was drawn in by James's likeability, apparent openness and ability (when not preoccupied with obtaining alcohol or dealing with the aftereffects) to interact with his children playfully and with warmth. However, very little had changed for this family, even though we had worked with them for a long time under child protection and in pre-proceedings. In fact, their situation was worsening.

'I think we should be offering James an opportunity to attend rehab', I said in supervision.

My manager asked, 'What makes you think that will work? Has he shown any indication of wanting to change?'

I hesitated, 'N...n..., ah, no', and provided several poorly reasoned explanations as to why I thought this should be pursued, nonetheless.

'Rich, why do you think you are asking this with this family? You seem to be overlooking the impact on the children, which is unlike you, and you're trying to offer James help when all of the evidence suggests he's not ready.'

She continued, 'I could understand it if there were some indicators of change, even small ones, but there are none.'

After a few moments in contemplation, I said, 'I just want him to have the help that I would want my dad to have had if he was in his position.'

My experiences growing up with my dad had some benefits in my practice. I never mixed up someone's morality or worth with their behaviour, even when they behaved in ways that were harmful for themselves or others around them. In working with James, I didn't judge him for using drugs, and I was empathetic to his inability to resolve his drug use, even though it was ruining his life and making his children unsafe. This helped our relationship even when I needed to have difficult conversations about his children being made subject to a child protection plan. The downside was that it created a blind spot that my manager was able to help me see.

Our experiences can help in many ways, but can also have harmful side effects. Acknowledging and making them conscious and explicit is one way to counteract these effects.

My approach to practice

Another feature of my upbringing that influenced my approach to social work was developing a compulsive caregiving strategy. I applied this, a strategy that had helped me in childhood, to social work. In fact, perhaps I sought social work out as a profession because I could use it – I had found a profession where I could, in theory, help others. Dr Patricia Crittenden and Dr Andrea Landini, authors of *Assessing Adult Attachment*, write 'by adulthood, compulsive caregivers feel safest and most comfortable when caring for other people, even to the exclusion of their own needs' (2011, p.155).

Furthermore, child protection social work's highly demanding and intense nature was a helpful distraction from myself. I formed an identity as a self-sacrificing, hard-working individual within the care profession. In her book *Our Inner Conflicts*, German psychoanalyst Dr Karen Horney suggests, 'a person builds up an idealized image of himself because he cannot tolerate himself as he actually is' (1945, p.112).

To add to this, in the same way I had moulded myself to elicit my mum's approval, I desperately sought my manager's approval, believing my worth was tied to my performance rather than anything intrinsic about myself. My desire to help children, coupled with a strategy that involved desperately seeking the approval of my manager, motivated by underlying feelings of worthlessness, were powerful drivers that propelled me to improve relentlessly.

One benefit of this strategy was that I could tolerate high levels of stress, in part because I suppressed my feelings. It wasn't that I didn't experience stress, but I didn't allow myself to acknowledge it or share it with those around me. Another benefit was that being attentive to the needs of others and adapting my response to minimize negative interactions was also an essential skill in working with children and families, especially when stakes and emotions were high.

The disadvantages, however, were that I could appear more confident and less stressed than I truly was. There were also personal costs to the strategy, namely, that I avoided emotional intimacy due to my association of intimacy with pain and rejection. Working in child protection gave me the perfect excuse, indeed, moral justification, to work long hours. And when I wasn't working, I was either preoccupied or exhausted.

Empathizing with parents

Learning about my upbringing and the strategy I developed has helped me understand my motivations as a social worker. It has also helped me understand and relate to the challenges parents I worked with faced when trying to change. The self-protective strategy I developed had helped me tremendously in childhood and created some benefits in adulthood. But it also hindered my ability to form intimate relationships with others.

Before learning about Crittenden's DMM, I was completely unaware I even had a strategy and could not change it. Fortunately for me, this strategy didn't cause my children to suffer significant harm. However, some parents I have worked with have developed a strategy that does cause harm, and they don't always realize it.

Finding out about the strategy was not a comfortable experience as I had to acknowledge the feelings from my childhood. I was also scared of letting go of the protective casing that, while keeping me disconnected from experiencing life fully, shielded my psyche from conscious awareness of the pain, hurt and feeling of rejection I had experienced as a child. Over many years, and with the benefit of a lot of therapy, I have achieved this.

In contrast, parents I worked with were asked to change involuntarily, at a speed that was often psychologically unmanageable, and without a supportive infrastructure. The way social work operates makes me wonder sometimes whether we have unconsciously and uncritically drunk at the behaviourist well of famous American psychologist B.F. Skinner – Skinner (1953) was of the view that behaviour that is punished will reduce and behaviour that is not, or is positively reinforced, will increase.

For example, we ask parents to sign written agreements requiring them to stop a whole host of behaviours and we outline the negative consequences should they not stop. Problems such as substance misuse and interpersonal violence, however, can sometimes have important self-protective functions (like my strategy, which protected me from negative feelings). In other words, the behaviours that we consider a problem may, in fact, be a parent's attempt at solving another problem (e.g., drug use solves psychological distress or loneliness).

In statutory social work, we must be clear about behaviour that is causing harm to children, and advocate for a reduction in that behaviour. We should also recognize that change is tough, even when the behaviour is causing harm to the self or others, and that simply asking someone not to do a behaviour or punishing them for it is unlikely to effect change.

Bringing awareness of our own experience of change may not drastically alter our approach to child protection, but it might substantially increase our empathy and compassion for parents who are being asked to change or who are in the process of changing, thereby enabling us to be realistic about the support and time required to make those changes.

Conclusion

Despite social work being a profession that professes the importance of self-reflexivity, it can feel taboo to reflect and connect our own journey with care and love (Andrew Turnell, personal communication, 2024). We like to say the words 'lived experience' but rarely talk about our own, and for some reason, we divorce the personal from the professional.

However, most of us have experienced adversity. And for many of us, this has contributed to our decision to work in the helping profession. I believe this is positive, but it comes with a responsibility, namely, cultivating self-reflection to allow for an ongoing evaluation of how these experiences might impact our work with children and families.

I decided to start with my experiences growing up to illustrate how our experiences can influence our practice as social workers.

This also allowed me to explore key concepts that will be expanded on throughout the book, such as attachment, developmental trauma, making personal change, addiction, mental health and personal values. In the following chapter, I will share key insights from my work with children who have experienced harm, and discuss how these lessons have shaped my approach to supporting both them and their families.

CHAPTER 2

Working with Children

THE POLICE ATTENDED A HOME after a neighbour contacted them and reported that they had heard shouting and screaming late at night. In the police report, it said,

> Arrived at property at 00:12, victim 21-year-old female, Lianne Watson, answered the door, holding Jacob, her two-year-old son. Victim upset and distressed. Said she argued with male suspect and partner, Gary Oldham. Suspect was angry, left while swearing denying he had done anything. After suspect left, we spoke to victim who didn't want to prosecute.

By the time I visited them two days later, Lianne and Gary presented as a unified couple, committed to their relationship with one another. They described the stress of looking after Jacob and his three-month-old sister Ella with little family support, and recalled difficult experiences growing up. They told me they had hated school, often being bullied and having few friends. Lianne said she fell for Gary when he stood up for her as a group of girls were making fun of her at the bus stop after school. After that, Gary said they were inseparable. They didn't care what others thought of them. Sometimes they would 'bunk' off school together and wander around, smoking cigarettes by the river and listening to music on shared headphones.

They both got jobs in a local supermarket, and, with money in their pockets, they said this was the best time of their lives. When Lianne got pregnant at 17, they were excited, dreaming of having a happy family together. When I asked about the police report, they said they had argued about the night feed, and there was confusion about whose turn it was. Jacob was awake and didn't seem affected, and Ella was asleep the whole time.

I left the visit feeling sorry for the parents. Lianne had a sense of futility born out of a life where others had mistreated her, leaving her feeling powerless to change it, whereas Gary presented as deeply insecure about whether others would be there for him. This, coupled with Gary's inability to handle strong feelings, meant he was defensive and inclined to misread situations, and he acted angrily and aggressively. Both parents, however, were desperate to try and afford their children the upbringing neither had had themselves.

I wrote up the assessment a few days later. I believed that because Jacob was young and Ella had been asleep, that the effects of witnessing or hearing their parents shout and argue would be negligible. I said their age was a protective factor because neither would remember this incident or have the language to describe what had happened.

My manager read the report. While I sat at my desk, she walked over with the report in her hand and pulled a chair around to sit beside me. Receiving feedback on my assessments always invoked anxiety. I put a lot of effort into writing an assessment, so it was always uncomfortable and difficult for me to learn about the many errors in terms of format, grammar or content. When we reached the section in the report about Jacob and Ella where I had written that their young age protected them from the effects of domestic abuse, my manager asked me, 'What did you mean by this?'

'Wasn't it obvious?' I thought to myself, trying to conceal my confusion by the question. 'Oh, um, I guess that Jacob and Ella are so young they probably aren't aware of what happened, so this kind of protected them.' If they were older, I could understand the query because they would know what had happened and then be able to talk about it and remember it when they were older.

Now it was my manager's turn to look confused; unlike me, however, she didn't hide it. She said, with encouragement, 'I would suggest taking a look at some of the research on how domestic abuse can impact on infants, then we can re-think it.'

This feedback from my manager was a formative moment for me. I assumed that children were not affected by domestic abuse because they were too young. When my manager questioned me on this, I went on a journey to learn about the impact of early experiences on brain development. This chapter is about that journey and how my understanding of children's development evolved. I also explore the limitations of what I learned and how this led me to look elsewhere into attachment theory and the implications this had for my practice.

Brain development

Initially, I learned about brain development in childhood. In their engrossing book, *The Boy Who Was Raised as a Dog*, psychiatrist Dr Bruce Perry and journalist Maria Szalavitz (2017) weave together insights from neuroscience with captivating case studies to describe how the brain undergoes significant development during infancy.

Perry and Szalavitz describe how the brain develops sequentially and from the bottom up. The brainstem, responsible for essential regulatory functions, develops in utero and early infancy. The midbrain and limbic systems develop next, rapidly developing in the first few years. The cortex, the most evolutionary recent and sophisticated part of the brain responsible for abstract thought, emotional regulation and planning, develops in adolescence and doesn't finish developing until well into adulthood.[1]

Perry and Szalavitz point out that a baby's responsiveness to its environment during this stage allows the baby to grow quickly, but

---

[1] The brain is astonishingly complex, and developments in neuroscience constantly change our understanding, often adding more nuance and complexity. While I think, as social workers, we can benefit from this knowledge, I don't have the technical knowledge and skills to rigorously interrogate the validity of a lot of it. Therefore, I have shared learning from one book on the topic and how I have used some of the ideas to inform my practice.

also makes the baby vulnerable to negative experiences. This means that adversity or a traumatic experience can impact a child differently, depending on their age.

Chronic and severe exposure to trauma early in infancy can alter the systems that regulate essential functions, and this can create lasting problems with physiological arousal (e.g., eating, toileting, sleeping, attachment, etc.) and emotional regulation. In turn, developmental capabilities that follow on from this as the child gets older, such as socialization, turn-taking and reading, can be harder to achieve or undermined by disruptions in essential arousal. A house built on shaky foundations is an overused yet helpful analogy here.

Alternatively, if a child has a stable start, with loving, attentive caregivers, and is then exposed to difficulties in middle childhood or adolescence, this will have a different impact because the brain is at a different stage of development. The effect of these disruptions will depend on the type of harm, duration, severity and availability of attentive, caring adults in the child's life.

This perspective had significant implications for my practice, especially later in my career, when I was involved in care proceedings and I had to support children in transitioning and adjusting to foster care. For example, a few years after I read Perry and Szalavitz's book, I was the social worker for Jack. Jack was an adorable six-year-old well-built boy with curly brown hair and big, round, brown eyes. He could be mischievous and energetic, and at times, showed very challenging behaviours that wreaked havoc for his foster carers, Marie and Andy. They were besotted with him but were exhausted because he had so much energy and would have 'massive meltdowns' over tiny things.

Marie and Andy were frustrated about Jack's difficulty in doing what other six-year-old children could do, such as getting along with other children, listening to instructions, engaging in joint play, concentrating for short periods and learning some basic self-care skills. These behaviours also affected him in school. Although Marie and Andy understood – theoretically – that the serious and frightening incidents of violence between his parents, frequent police callouts and the emotional abuse from his mum had affected Jack's development and ability to trust others, they struggled to know what to do differently. I was also at a loss.

My job involved assessing harm to a child, a parent's capacity to change and making difficult recommendations. I felt ill equipped and out of my depth offering therapeutic parenting advice. In the midst of this, I remembered Perry's idea of the neurosequential model of therapeutics, which he observed in one of the foster carers he worked with, called 'Mama P.'

> When Mama P. had rocked and held the traumatized children she cared for, she'd intuitively discovered what would become the foundation of our neuro-sequential approach: these children need patterned, repetitive experiences appropriate to their developmental needs that reflect the age which they'd missed important stimuli or had been traumatized, not their chronological age. (Perry and Szalavitz 2017, p.152)

In reflecting on this idea with Marie and Andy, we discussed how they could care for Jack in a way that compensated for the lack of soothing, repetitive, rhythmic and connected experiences during his infancy. Marie started taking him to baby massage, sing and sign and baby swimming classes; chronologically, he was the oldest in these classes by a large margin, but developmentally, he fitted in. Marie and Andy also changed his evening routine, treating him like a much younger child, having a bath every night, rocking and singing nursery rhymes to him.

Did this solve all of Jack's emotional and behavioural problems? Unfortunately not. There are no solutions that provide perfect outcomes in social work, a painful lesson that I learned over and over again. But it did reduce the intensity of Jack's 'meltdowns', helped Marie and Andy feel more confident, and improved their relationship enough to prevent it from breaking down.

Memory

Returning to Jacob and Ella, contrary to the view I had formed, infants and young children are far from being protected by their young age; rather, they are more vulnerable to adversity and stress. Further, I had assumed that Jacob and Ella would not be affected because when they were older they wouldn't be able to recall or remember what had happened.

The truth was, although Jacob and Ella would have no explicit verbal memory, the memories of uncomforted fear and distress when their parents had argued could be stored in their body and brain. Clinical Professor of Psychiatry and author of several books, Dr Dan Siegel, writes, in *The Developing Mind*, 'Our earliest experiences shape our ways of behaving, including patterns of relating to others, without our ability to recall consciously when these first learning experiences occurred' (1999, p.24).

If anything, their inability to recall and use language to explain meant they would have no awareness of what had caused their fears and responses. Later in life, they might experience automatic reactions based on these past experiences with no understanding or ability to articulate why they behaved the way they did. They wouldn't be able to use language to explain to others what had happened and how it made them feel, or to receive help from others to make sense of it.

Memory is not like a tidy filing drawer, where memories are neatly organized and easily retrievable, which we can then share with others like it's a photo or a video (Baim and Morrison 2011). Instead, it's more akin to a jam-packed filing cabinet. The bottom drawers hold our earliest experiences and loads of other stuff that's buried deep in our unconscious, practically locked away. The top drawer, though, is accessible – it's where we keep the memories we can recall, although they might not always be totally reliable. Plus, every time we pull out a memory, we kind of tweak it a bit when we describe it. This leads to two main types of memory – implicit and explicit.

Implicit memory is unconscious and non-verbal. It includes emotional and bodily-based memories as well as procedural memory (i.e., learned skills), and it disproportionately influences our behaviour.

Explicit memory, on the other hand, is conscious and verbal, and can recall events, facts and general knowledge. Neuroscientist, author and science communicator David Eagleman writes in his book *Incognito: The Secret Lives of the Brain*, 'the first thing we learn from studying our own circuitry is a simple lesson: most of what we do and think and feel is not under our conscious control' (2011, p.4).

Attachment theory

Alongside learning about brain development, I began another journey (which is ongoing) to learn about attachment theory. Learning about brain development had shifted my perspective on how profound early experiences were on early development, but I struggled to use my new knowledge to make sense of the multitude of behaviours I was observing in all the children (and adults) I was working with.

Tianna, a 14-month-old chubby baby with light, wispy hair that revealed dry, scaly skin and a noticeable flat head lived with her parents, Deanne and David. Deanne and David were a pleasure to work with. They were always welcoming, amenable and very loving towards Tianna. However, they had a problem – a serious heroin and crack cocaine addiction.

Deanne, despite her addiction, took great pride in her appearance. However, her pale complexion and the dark, weary bags under her eyes spoke to the emotional and physical strain she was under. David, unlike Deanne, had lost interest in looking after himself. With scruffy brown hair, he was painfully slim, had few teeth, and his vacant eyes were set within a gaunt, yellow face. Although their home was clean and tidy, it was also musty and dark, and sparsely furnished, with few toys for Tianna.

During visits, I would sit on the thread-torn, rouge sofa that felt like it would swallow me up if I sat too far back into it. As I spoke about the recent incidents – Deanne had been caught by security stealing in the local Morrisons using Tianna's buggy; a neighbour had reported that they had heard Deanne and David shouting and screaming at each other in the early hours of the morning; David had been observed with a can of lager walking Tianna to the nursery – I would watch as Tianna sat there quietly, like an old lady sat on a park bench, peacefully watching life pass by. Tianna was a passive baby, placing few demands on her parents, and she played on her own, albeit in a rudimentary and basic way. There wasn't much playing in her play.

Occasionally, I would turn to Tianna, smile exaggeratedly, widen my eyes, and speak in that high-pitched way we instinctively do when talking to young children. Like turning on a light switch, her face would light up, her eyes would spring to life, and she would smile broadly. But her facial expression evaporated when my attention returned to Deanne and David, who were providing some convoluted, semi-believable explanation that would discredit the recent concern.

I was puzzled by this discrepancy. Tianna presented as being largely unaffected by what was happening and appeared capable of entertaining herself with few signs of distress. When I interacted with her, she reacted positively. Yet she was being cared for by two parents who heavily misused substances, rendering them emotionally unavailable – and sometimes physically unavailable, too – as testified by the chronology (see Chapter 5).

Only after reading *Raising Parents* by Dr Patricia Crittenden (2008) would I understand Tianna's presentation. A basic premise of the dynamic-maturational model of attachment and adaptation (DMM), which developed out of the work of John Bowlby and Mary Ainsworth,[2] is that as we grow, our development is influenced by our

---

2 Bowlby developed the theory and Ainsworth provided the empirical data to support the theory. They developed three basic patterns, ABC. However, there was another group of children who didn't fit those three patterns. Two of Ainsworth's students, Mary Main and Patricia Crittenden, developed different ideas about how to conceptualize the behaviour of these children, which led to a split in attachment theory. Crittenden developed the DMM, which I refer to in this book because I have found it the most useful in my work. Main and her colleagues developed and added the 'disorganized/disorientated' category to Ainsworth's original ABC (avoidant, secure, ambivalent) classification, and this model has been widely accepted and often taught on social work programmes. For an overview of the DMM, including how it differs from the ABC+D model (+ disorganized), see Landa and Duschinsky (2013).

experiences and relationships, especially with our primary caregiver. Attachment is what happens between the child and an attachment figure, usually a parent.

According to attachment theory, an infant is born with a relatively limited repertoire of behaviours to elicit care from adult caregivers, such as vocalizing, grimacing and crying. As they grow older, the repertoire expands, and they can use behaviours such as talking, shouting, caressing or cuddling to alert their caregivers when they are in need. Therefore, these 'attachment' behaviours help an infant get their needs met *and* keep their caregiver close. When a caregiver reliably provides comfort and protection, the infant learns to trust their feelings, communicate with others about them, and rely on others for care and comfort when needed. They develop a secure attachment, or, in DMM terms, they use a balanced Type B strategy.[3]

However, not all infants are afforded this level of care by their caregivers. Throughout a human history characterized by extreme poverty, an absence of healthcare, welfare system or education provision, high rates of child mortality, war, genocides and a plethora of natural disasters (Pinker 2018), the vulnerable infant has had to find ways to get the best care possible from caregivers who might be affected by these issues to ensure their survival. More contemporary issues such as domestic abuse, substance misuse and mental health affect parental availability in similar ways and necessitate adaptation for survival.

When an infant's experiences lead them to distrust a caregiver, like when communicating about their distress directly fails to elicit care, they must find different ways to deal with their distress and communicate it in such a way that maximizes their chances of getting some comfort or protection. Over time, the child learns (implicitly) how to get the best care available from their caregivers, and a pattern of relating emerges. For these children, categorized as either

---

3   Individuals using a Type B strategy feel comfortable seeking support and are generally able to express their emotions and needs appropriately. This strategy usually develops when caregivers are consistently responsive and nurturing, allowing the child to feel safe and secure.

Type A[4] or Type C,[5] their ways of thinking and feeling might be very different to those children who are fortunate enough to have caregivers who are reliably available to protect and comfort them (Type B).

These self-protective strategies are an impressive feat of human ingenuity that reflects an intrinsic resourcefulness that allows us to survive, even in suboptimal environments. For example, when some children call out using attachment behaviours, they may be ignored, rejected or handled roughly. In response, they learn to hide or inhibit the display of their feelings (Type A). Remarkably, even babies as young as two months old can learn not to cry if crying leads to negative reactions from their caregivers.

If every time a baby cried the caregiver didn't respond because they were depressed or using drugs, then, over time, the child might learn, 'expressing my feelings doesn't make any difference, it just makes me feel worse'. They might deny their needs and find ways to cut off processing the feelings from their body, such as hunger, discomfort and loneliness. This way, they don't use up all their energy crying when it makes no difference, but to do this, they have to find ways to try and cut off awareness of their bodily sensations and feelings.

Tianna's behaviours made much more sense when I learned about this. Tianna, having learned that her parents weren't always available to meet her emotional needs, switched off, and as a result, she became passive and disconnected. This created the false impression that she was unaffected.

---

4   Individuals using a Type A strategy tend to avoid seeking comfort or support from others; they often downplay their emotional needs and may appear independent and self-reliant. This strategy often arises in environments where caregivers are unresponsive or rejecting, causing the child to learn that expressing feelings and seeking help are not effective.

5   Those using a Type C strategy often exhibit ambivalence or resistance in relationships; they may feel insecure about the availability of support and often oscillate between seeking closeness and pushing others away. This strategy can manifest as clinginess or heightened anxiety in relationships, stemming from inconsistent caregiving. Children may have experienced caregivers who were unpredictably available, leading to confusion about whether their emotional needs will be met.

In the development of the DMM, Crittenden built on the work of Bowlby and Ainsworth to identify an expanding array of self-protective strategies available to humans across their lifespan. In the pre-school years, some children might pretend to be happy because they have discovered that although their parents can't tolerate displays of negative feelings, they get a positive response if they smile and appear happy. If they apply this strategy of being attentive to the needs of others and doing whatever pleases adults in school, they can excel and get positive feedback from their teachers. However, hidden from view are their true negative feelings of sadness, anger or desire for comfort.

Older children can develop strategies such as taking care of their parents by putting aside their emotional needs and focusing on meeting their parents' needs (the compulsive caregiving I, myself, developed). They may also comply with adults' expectations without complaining to avoid punishment or disapproval.

If these strategies don't work, that is, they don't reduce hostility or increase the attachment figure's availability, they might develop a do-it-by-yourself strategy (self-reliance) in adolescence. This is a strategy where negative feelings are cut off almost entirely, and the young person no longer depends on others for support, at least psychologically. Or the young person might become socially or sexually promiscuous as a way of experiencing intimacy without forming the emotional bonds that could lead to them being hurt or rejected.

Sometimes these children are described by the professionals working with them as 'resilient'. Over the years, I've encountered many children like Tianna, who appear to cope exceptionally well despite living in dire situations. I have observed it most in children who are chronically and pervasively neglected, where they have developed low expectations regarding their parents.

Knowing this hasn't always prevented me from being misled by some children. I have often been confused – how do you know if the child's apparent happiness is false or true? Crittenden laments the importance of identifying discrepancies and using them to uncover meaning. Tianna created a discrepancy for me. She was a young infant living with chronic, serious drug users, exposed to domestic abuse, criminal behaviour and neglectful care. Yet she did not appear to be outwardly affected. How could this be? Given everything we know about child development, it would be reasonable to assume there would be some adverse effects from her experiences.

I used this discrepancy to generate hypotheses and consider my next steps. It could be that Tianna was being offered compensatory care from other adults in her network, or she could have developed a self-protective strategy that hid her distress. Once I found out that Tianna's parents were isolated, I could rule out the possibility that she was receiving compensatory care, which further evidenced my assessment that Tianna had, in fact, developed a self-protective strategy of inhibiting the display of her feelings and downplaying her dependency needs.

Although not an exhaustive list, here are *some* behaviours associated with the Type A strategy:

- Eagerness to please (except when asked about feelings, especially negative ones) that can make the professional or caregiver feel good about interacting with them
- Refusal to speak negatively about caregivers or past experiences, or downplaying, denying, minimizing or leaving out the emotional effects
- Pausing before replying to a question (to monitor what they say and/or change what they think/feel)
- Dysfluent when talking about negative feelings, squirming in their chair, minimizing (she was a 'bit' scared, a 'bit' sad), or changing the subject
- Denying distress to self or taking responsibility for bad things happening
- Smiling or laughing when describing negative events
- Hypervigilant – being startled by sudden noises outside
- Limited playfulness, especially imaginative play
- Use of eye contact to check they are getting it 'right', or eye contact avoidance

- Sitting on hands, shaking knees, scratching, biting nails (to hide anxiety) while smiling (false positive affect).

Alternatively, in unpredictable caregiving contexts in which a child's display of anger, fear and desire for comfort are intermittently positively reinforced, children develop a different kind of strategy for self-protection.

Charlie was a slim, seven-year-old boy who was short for his age, had pale brown freckles on his cheeks, and wore large round glasses. 'Charlie, mate, can you please come and sit down while we look at this worksheet?' I asked him for the umpteenth time. 'It won't take long', I pleaded.

'How many times do you think I can spin around on this chair?' he replied as he spun around on the old office chair in the small cupboard-like room. A room with a small table, two chairs and various pieces of unused school supplies lying around (an old printer, a whiteboard, a large stationery cupboard and a hoover).

Before I had the chance to reply, he stood up on the chair and spun himself around faster and faster. He glanced back at me with a sly smirk and a glint in his eye. In this moment, there seemed to be a silent acknowledgement that Charlie knew he was doing something he shouldn't, and he eagerly awaited my reaction. He knew he had my attention; even better, it was on his terms.

I smiled, in part marvelling at the intelligence of his strategy, and in part because I didn't know what else to do. 'You are awesome at spinning around, shall we play that game we played last time?' I said, hiding my frustration that, once again, I wouldn't be able to do any meaningful direct work with him to be able to understand his wishes and feelings.

'Sure', he said. We played the game for several minutes before Charlie became restless and sabotaged it. Walking back to the class feeling dissatisfied, Charlie skipped up from behind me, shouting out quick-fire questions, such as, 'Are you going to see my mum now?', 'Will you see my sister after me?', 'When are you coming again?' and 'Can you come tomorrow?'

When he caught me up, he surprised me by taking hold of my hand as we walked along the school corridor, and at the doorway, he turned towards me, hugged my legs and bounced back into his classroom. My exasperation dissolved, and I left with warm feelings, 'He's such a sweet kid, really.'

Charlie seemed to have developed an opposite self-protective strategy to Tianna (i.e., a Type C strategy). Such a strategy arises from being cared for by attachment figures who sometimes respond positively, sometimes late (when the child is really upset or really angry), or not at all. The main feature is that the attachment figure is inconsistent, and intermittently positively reinforces the display of negative feelings. There could be various reasons for this, such as stressful life events and situations, mental health issues, substance misuse, domestic abuse and/or preoccupation with a partner or other children in the family. In this caregiving context, the child becomes anxious and learns they cannot rely on others to respond promptly and with comfort.

The infant developing a Type C strategy learns to cry louder and quicker to improve the chance they will get a response. Even when they get the comfort they need, anxiety arises about the attachment figure putting them down in case they can't get them back when they need them. As Clark Baim and Tony Morrison, authors of *Attachment-Based Practice with Adults*, put it, 'the child's strategy is twofold: exaggerate my negative feelings and keep the problem unsolvable' and 'the baby becomes fussy, complaining, and inconsolable, and thus begins the struggle of intense, inconsistent, intrusive and enmeshed mis-communication that may come to characterize future relationship patterns' (2011, p.35).

As the infant becomes a pre-schooler, they may escalate to more challenging behaviour, such as acts of physical aggression (hitting, kicking, throwing objects) or behaviour that forces a reaction, such as running away, climbing tables and window ledges, or having tantrums. When the child senses that the attachment figure is about to lose it (and withdraw or get angry), they switch to a vulnerable display, perhaps crying or looking sad and needy, which disarms the caregivers' frustration and draws them close again.

In the school years and during adolescence, these sorts of behavioural strategies might become even more dangerous, with criminal behaviour, school exclusions, violence against peers and teachers, substance misuse and sexual promiscuity.

In my experience, teenagers using this strategy can split professional networks. The young person might seem cheeky, charming, likeable, vulnerable and obviously in need, yet at the same time obtuse, aggressive or difficult. Some professionals might only see one side of the 'strategy' and find it difficult to believe the experience of other professionals. Although these alternations always co-exist, children using this strategy tend to rely on one side of the strategy more than the other.

The genius outcome is that children like Charlie behave unpredictably to make their caregivers more predictable. I first thought that if I could find a way to reduce Charlie's emotional and behavioural difficulties, the situation at home would improve. Once I realized that Charlie's behaviour was in response to his caregiving context, I could instead focus on helping his parents be more sensitive to his needs.

Charlie felt alone and was profoundly frightened without parental attention, so he worked hard to get it and keep it! The solution was not fixing Charlie but supporting his mum, Leila, to develop a context where Charlie could have more trust in receiving a reliable response from her. It gave me a different way to think about helping other families where children had developed this strategy.

Instead of focusing on the child, I focused on the sources of distraction for the parents, such as an addiction, domestically abusive relationship or their attachment strategy. As Crittenden points out, 'anxious attachment is good when parents are not sensitively responsive to an infant's needs; it is the child's contribution to his or her survival' and 'Danger is the problem...change the danger, not the child' (2016, p.33).

Here are some behaviours associated with the Type C strategy:

- Fluctuating from displaying anger, risk-taking behaviour and provocation (to elicit and sustain attention) to coy, vulnerable, 'rescue me' behaviour (to disarm adults while still doing what they want)
- Being cooperative until they become preoccupied with something else that interests them
- Unnecessarily moving stuff, mocking the task, making fun of adults, or the professional finds they are doing all the work
- Looking at the caregiver or professional before doing forbidden things (to see if they have pushed the limit too far)
- Exaggerating negative emotion ('really, really' sad, 'very, very' angry), and dismissing the feelings of others
- Memories and stories run on and on, meandering to where the child wants to go – talking without thinking
- Using evocative language to dramatize feelings or problems.

Working with children like Tianna and Charlie taught me how they can adapt to their caregiving context in a way that improves their caregiver's response and reduces risk. Children are responsive to their environments. This doesn't mean they are responsible, but it does mean that the social worker needs to situate the children's emotional and behavioural presentation within their context.

Tianna and Charlie didn't realize that they had moulded themselves; they just did it. Like breathing or walking. They had both learned the most efficient way of responding to their parents early in life. When behaviour is learned early, it becomes an engrained way of responding, and it increases the chance that it will be used in other contexts where it is not needed, such as at school. In other words, what helps children in one context at a particular time might be used in another context or later in their life in unhelpful ways.

For example, if Tianna continued to grow up in an environment pervasively lacking in comfort and protection, she might develop a compulsively promiscuous strategy and look for love, affection and intimacy outside of the home with unfamiliar others, not allowing herself to get too close for too long. Although she would be reducing the chances of feeling the pain, rejection, feelings of worthlessness and shame that she had experienced in the past in close relationships, there is a risk of exploitation, disease, pregnancy and violence.

By taking the time to understand the underlying function of Tianna's behaviour, we might be better able to help. Recognizing her profound fear of genuine intimacy and her desperate need for affection could redirect efforts away from educating her about the risks of such behaviour towards identifying ways to help her find alternative means of securing affection and intimacy.

On a final note, the DMM is a dynamic model. That is, self-protective strategies are not fixed and are contingent on the environment. There are opportunities for change and adaptation throughout childhood (and, as I can attest, adulthood!). A child's situation may stabilize, leading to greater balance, or worsen, leading to the development of a more extreme self-protective strategy.

Conclusion

Like any good manager, when my supervisor noticed I had mistakenly believed that children were protected from adversity due to their age, she didn't simply correct me and tell me why. Instead, she highlighted where I had gone wrong and encouraged me to find this out myself. Understanding brain development, even at a rudimentary level, changed my perspective on the impact of harm on infants. Following that, I learned how children can adapt to their caregiving context.

The greater the harm children experience, the more sophisticated the strategy needs to be, and in turn, the greater the risk of problems later in life. One of my most important lessons was that in the absence of danger, children could adapt to various parenting techniques and approaches and be at low risk of developing problems later in life. This reorientated my approach in helping children and families – away from fixing the child or supporting the parent to improve parenting skills and knowledge towards identifying and reducing the impact of critical dangers.

In our work, key dangers include domestic abuse, substance misuse, mental health and neglect. Arguably, therefore, any intervention that is aimed at improving outcomes in a child's life should prioritize minimizing the danger within the family.

In subsequent chapters, I will explore how we, as social workers, can help parents reduce danger. But before we move on to working with parents, I will explore the importance of direct work with children.

CHAPTER 3

Working Directly with Children

U NDERTAKING DIRECT WORK WITH CHILDREN can be the most rewarding part of being a social worker. Yet it can also be the most challenging. Simple in theory, hard in practice. Before jumping into some of the challenges and outlining some principles I have found useful over the years, it's worth distinguishing between the two types of direct work we are often asked to do in child protection:

- *To ascertain the wishes and feelings of a child,* to discover a child's worries, anxieties, hopes and wishes, to understand how they've made sense of their world. This could be as part of an assessment under Section 17 of the Children Act 1989 (voluntary) or an ongoing feature of our work – for example, if the child is subject to a child protection plan or a Child in Care.
- *A therapeutic piece of work to help children understand their experiences,* especially those that have warranted social work involvement, such as exposure to domestic abuse, parental mental ill health and substance misuse.

These are two different yet interlinked aspects of our direct work with children. When I first qualified, I tended to focus on the first. However, over the years, I realized that part of my role was to help children understand the reason for my involvement, so I started to look for ways to help me explain difficult subjects to children.

Challenges of direct work

This process was filled with challenges I needed to overcome.

Protecting a child's innocence

First, there is a society-wide unwritten agreement that exists to preserve and protect children from adult issues. My friend and social worker, Andy Black, described this in a post on my blog in 2020: 'Childhood is conceptualized as a sacred and discrete time of life that should be protected. It is, therefore, socially acceptable and preferred to actively protect children from the often-harsh realities of adult life, and in some cases, lie to them to preserve preconceived notions of innocence.'

However, in child protection, the unfortunate reality is that I would only become involved in a child's life if someone was concerned for them. I was, therefore, visiting children suspected of being harmed, or where this had already been established, and so I would work with them on an ongoing basis. Either way, I had to speak to children about topics I wouldn't usually discuss with them – conversations about violence, mental health, death, loss, drug and alcohol misuse, criminal behaviour, sexual abuse, physical abuse, and so on.

The founder of Signs of Safety,[1] Andrew Turnell, and consultant family therapist, Susie Essex, in their superb book, *Working with Denied Child Abuse*, captured my experience of this as a newly qualified social worker: 'Professionals, perhaps informed by an overly sentimental view of childhood innocence are often at a loss regarding how to communicate the enormity of the events to children caught up in situations of abuse' (2006, p.72).

A key realization I came to was that whatever I thought I was protecting the children from, they had already lived through it. I was

---

1   www.signsofsafety.net/what-is-sofs

avoiding topics such as mum and dad fighting, dad drinking alcohol and mum being depressed out of some sense that a child shouldn't be exposed to such topics. Yet in some cases, this was their day-to-day reality.

One of the most interesting findings I have learned of recently was from James Pennebaker, Professor Emeritus of Psychology, who has studied extensively the link between expressive writing and emotional and physical health outcomes (Pennebaker and Smyth 2016). He argued that not discussing – or writing about – a traumatic or distressing experience can have a more significant effect, emotionally and physically, than the experience itself. In other words, a traumatic event is bad for your health, and if you keep that trauma a secret, it may have an even worse impact.

Psychiatrist Dr Bessel van der Kolk, in his *New York Times* best-selling book on trauma, *The Body Keeps the Score*, put it this way:

> Feeling listened to and understood changes our physiology... As long as you keep secrets and suppress information, you are fundamentally at war with yourself. Hiding your core feelings takes an enormous amount of energy...stress hormones keep flooding your body, leading to headaches, muscle aches, problems with your bowels or sexual functions – and irrational behaviours that may embarrass you and hurt others. (2014, p.233)

Time to build trust and overcome fear

The second challenge I faced was dealing with the sheer volume of work that was expected of me. I struggled to plan direct work sessions with children and spend enough time building trust with them; I had to find ways of building trust and rapport quickly. Related to this, visiting children in their homes also presented challenges – it was awkward when I sat in a bedroom speaking to a child about their mum or dad, knowing they were potentially within earshot.

Furthermore, when I visited children, I would also have to speak to the parents, observe the family together, and check out the home conditions – all before I had to rush off to my next meeting. In a paper by Professor of Social Work Harry Ferguson, titled 'How children become invisible in child protection work', he found that some social workers were effective with some children in eliciting the child's wishes and feelings, yet the same social worker might struggle with a child in a different home as they would be 'overcome by the sheer complexity of the interactions they encounter, the emotional intensity of the work, parental resistance and the tense atmospheres in the homes', and this could result in them 'unintentionally losing sight of the child' (Ferguson 2017, p.1017).

In other words, certain families can cause certain responses in social workers that could disable their skills in their direct work with children. I've certainly worked with parents where I have been scared walking up to their house, and hoped they would not answer due to fear and apprehension. If I had acted on these feelings, that would have meant not seeing the child.

Feeling comfortable with difficult conversations

Third, talking about the topics I encountered in child protection was sometimes personally difficult and uncomfortable. Even when I could overcome the impulse to protect children from 'adult' topics and create enough space and time to spend with them, my unease could prevent me from asking questions or exploring certain issues, especially around the topic of sexual abuse. Systemic psychotherapist John Burnham (2018) described an experience that illustrated this. He was working with a woman who he thought was avoiding why she was attending therapy – which was because of her experience of sexual abuse:

> 'Every time we approach that issue, you seem to change the subject... I am wondering why?' As I began to speak the question, I changed it to, 'Every time we approach that issue, the conversation goes somewhere else. Who do you think avoids it more...me or you?'
>
> My thinking was still influenced by the idea that she was avoiding, but I wanted to be kinder by including myself in the question.
>
> She replied, 'you do'.

I was taken aback, but eventually received curiosity to enquire 'How? What do I do?... How do you notice that?'

Thankfully she replied, 'Well, whenever I am close to talking about what happened you will say something like 'It doesn't have to be now...take your time and so on.'

Burnham reflected, 'in my wish to be sensitive I had acted superficially' (2018, p.17).

So often, my discomfort about a particular topic would lead me to avoid it, thus denying the child the chance to talk about it. Of course, some children might not want to talk about sensitive issues, and as social workers, we should respect that. But that's different from them not being given the chance because I felt awkward, embarrassed or nervous. Learning to be comfortable exploring these topics is not easy, but I have found it is possible through practice and using some tools to provide a structure to have these difficult conversations.

In the following section, I will draw together the lessons that shaped my approach to undertaking direct work or completing a visit to a child before sharing an approach that changed how I communicated to children about their adverse experiences.

Establishing the purpose of direct work

When I first qualified, I thought it was my job to extract from children their views on the issues that had led to my involvement with them. If I left a visit with a child without succeeding, which was nearly all the time, I felt like a failure.

Blaming yourself is sometimes a useful strategy because it causes you to reflect on how you did something, and whether there are different and better ways of approaching a task. However, in this instance, it wasn't just that I was approaching it wrongly, which I was, but that my expectations for what was realistic were also wrong. In other words, I misunderstood the purpose.

My job was not to make children talk about their experiences, but instead to maximize their opportunity to do so if they wanted to.

That is a very different goal. I often left visits with children with a ton of information about them, but none of the information was relevant for the purposes of my involvement with them. For example, I could visit a seven-year-old girl and know her favourite food, colour, TV programme, best friend, best lesson, worst lesson, favourite teacher and much more, yet I would have no idea how she had felt about the police coming around to her house the night before when they arrested her dad after he had violently assaulted her older brother. She wasn't going to bring it into the conversation, and when I first started as a newly qualified social worker, I certainly wasn't going to – let's instead talk and draw about happy and safe topics, pretending everything is okay.

I have since learned various techniques that have helped me to feel comfortable and confident in having such difficult conversations with children. In my experience, children have a strong detector for assessing whether I am trustworthy, sensitive and able to handle their thoughts and feelings. If a child senses that I am nervous or apprehensive talking, for example, about their mum and dad fighting or taking drugs, they will instinctively withdraw and withhold sharing anything with me, whatever technique I am using.

The child has to feel safe – psychologically and relationally – and that is tied to how confident I feel in navigating the relationship with them. Therefore, while certain techniques improved my communication skills, the greatest benefit was that they helped me feel more confident, and that, more than anything, is what children respond to.

Practice builds ability

I have worked with many social workers who appear innately capable of skilfully and sensitively building relationships with children. Usually, they could engender the sense of trust with children that I just mentioned as being crucial. I was not granted such innate skills.

Fortunately for us in the struggling but eager-to-learn camp, I believe that direct work is a skill that can be learned and developed.

I did plenty of direct work with children during my final placement – during my first few years as a social worker, I had a manager who encouraged, if not expected, me to undertake six sessions of direct work with every child I worked for. There were three valuable lessons from these experiences.

First, I found that children were unbelievably forgiving of my flaws and inadequacies as long as they trusted my intention of genuine curiosity. Second, it was okay to experiment with different worksheets and tools – I didn't need to worry about ensuring that I had the exact worksheet given the child's age and interests. I also realized that a worksheet that worked wonders for a six-year-old boy could fail miserably with a six-year-old girl, or what worked for an eight-year-old didn't work for a ten-year-old. Third, later in my career, when I needed to visit children in urgent circumstances, I could condense the relationship and trust building that typically occurred over several weeks into less than an hour. **This did all take considerable practice, however**.

Introductions with children

As a newly qualified social worker visiting children, I was so preoccupied with my feelings that it would escape me that the child would enter into the room with their own set of worries, expectations and feelings. It didn't occur to me for some time that a child would bring their own feelings and ideas about the purpose of my visit. What did they think or know about the reason I was visiting? Did they think I was there to find out how naughty they had been? Because they were in trouble? To find out things and tell their parents? To punish or trick them?

Kayleigh Llewellyn created the critically acclaimed TV drama series *In My Skin*. In an interview with Professor of Social Work Donald Forrester, she described her experience of growing up in a family home with severe mental ill health and domestic violence, and how these had influenced the themes covered in her BAFTA award-winning drama (Forrester 2022). At one point Forrester asked about how professionals could support a child, like herself, growing up with those issues, and her reply illuminates the challenges children face in opening up:

> I was a teenager in late 90s and early noughties so it's quite a different landscape I imagine to how things would be in a school to now, um my biggest fear growing up was that a social worker would become involved in my life, um, one because I had the feeling that if a social worker was involved I would simply be taken away from my mum, I didn't know that there was a different level of involvement, it was like, if they know, you'll be taken away, which I didn't want, um and probably isn't the reality of the situation but as a kid that is what you think, um, I also would not have wanted the stigma, like, the feeling, because I was so afraid this information would get out to my peers, the idea that a social worker might be involved makes it even more likely that this news might get out and how much more damning that would be, I thought anyway. Um, so maybe that boils down to sort of, yeah, I wish I had known more about it, more than I maybe saw on the odd drama or tv and what it is for a social worker to be involved, should know more about what roles a social worker, um can fulfil and how they might have been able to help in terms of what people could of done to help me.

I realized that explaining my role and the reason for my visit would be one of the most effective ways to alleviate the concerns described by Kayleigh Llewellyn that many of the children I worked with experienced, although this was not straightforward. In my first few years, I often felt unsure about what I was doing – I couldn't explain what I was doing to myself, never mind explaining it to a six-year-old.

After attending some training with Rob Tucker, the most skilled and knowledgeable practitioner I have encountered on the topic of direct work with children, I took on board his advice and developed a script that I have used ever since:

My name is Rich, and I'm a social worker. Have you had a social worker before?

If you have, can you tell me why that was and what they did?

What do you think a social worker does? There is no right or wrong answer. I am interested in knowing what you think.

I am a children's social worker, so I work with mums, dads and children. But social workers don't work with all children. We only work with children when there might be some worries about what's happening in their family. Can you tell me what worries you think people might have about you or your family? If you had to guess?

Social workers work with children and their families for lots of different reasons, like when mums and dads argue a lot, if someone is really unwell, if mums or dads are taking drugs or drinking alcohol, if an adult has touched a child in their private parts, or if parents are finding it hard to look after their children. Do you think anyone has these worries about you? Can you tell me more about that?

If the child doesn't answer, I would tell them the reason for social work involvement, and then ask, 'Can you tell me more about that?'

Sometimes I would explain to them that my job is to write a report:

My job is to write a report about your mum and dad and how they look after you. Have you received a school report? In your school report, your teacher will give you feedback on how you are doing with writing, reading, numbers and other subjects. You might be doing well in some subjects, and less well in others. Well, in the same way your teacher writes a report about you in school, I am writing a report about mum and dad and how they are doing. As part of this report, I will speak to lots of people, like mum, dad, some family members and your teacher, to find out what your life is like, but the most important person I need to speak to is you. Afterwards, I write a report and see if there are some areas that mum and dad might need support with – how does that sound to you?

Using these questions and script helped me feel more confident, often reducing the child's fears and cultivating trust and a platform from which we could have meaningful discussions.

How to structure a visit

There were a few techniques that helped me structure and navigate a session with a child. First, I adopted the use of four phases, as outlined in the 'Achieving Best Evidence' (ABE) guidance for police officers and other trained professionals interviewing children and vulnerable adults about allegations of abuse (Ministry of Justice 2022).

This guidance provides a formula for conducting each session or interview: (1) Establishing rapport; (2) Initiating and supporting a free narrative account; (3) Questioning; and (4) Closure. I would begin each session establishing rapport (or re-establishing it) by exploring neutral topics, and then transition into encouraging a discussion about the reason for my visit (see the script above), following up with specific questions, and then concluding by returning to trivial issues or something playful.

Second, there are two communication techniques. Tell, Explain and Describe (TED) is a helpful acronym to aid in asking open-ended questions. The other technique is paraphrasing, a technique I've been guilty of overusing.

'Why do you just keep repeating everything I say', an astute, feisty, 14-year-old girl said to me once. She probably picked up on the fact I was covering up my insecurity with one technique. Reflecting to children what they've just said, with raised intonation at the end, encourages them to share more without asking a question.

Reflecting back to children their emotions and actions can also be effective (e.g., 'You looked like you were about to say something then, and you stopped yourself', 'You looked uncomfortable when I asked you about your dad', 'Your face changed when I asked about mum's drinking and you looked sad'). Even when children don't answer these reflections, if accurate, they can be powerful ways of affirming or acknowledging a child's emotional experience.

Third, was to have fun with children. I took my job too seriously initially, but having fun is one of the most effective ways to build a relationship. Some of the best direct work I have done with children or young people has been while I've been sat next to them playing FIFA on their games console or playing basketball outside. It is known that physical play can be incredibly effective, as it can change the physiological state of the child and activate their 'social engagement system' (Porges 2017, p.22), making them more capable of engaging in dialogue.

Responding well to challenges

The two biggest challenges I have faced have been children who were unwilling to share their worries out of fear of repercussions, and children who have developed coping strategies that prevent them from engaging in conversation. In the first instance, where the child is reticent, I have to remind myself that the goal is not to make the child talk, but to maximize the chance of them sharing their thoughts and feelings.

I met Jenny, a 10-year-old girl, at her small primary school one autumn morning. She had brown, unbrushed and greasy hair that was tied up loosely. She walked in with her head bowed, her gaze fixed on her feet, each step a deliberate and measured movement. Her white collar had turned grey, mirroring the colour that had drained from her face. Her shoes held onto her feet with threadbare laces and holes in the front. Avoiding eye contact, she sat down slowly and placed her hands on her lap as she fiddled with her nails. I felt a pang of discomfort, as if I was about to prod a wounded animal. Part of me wanted to leave, 'Surely this isn't very fair on her, she's clearly uncomfortable', trying to soothe myself that if I did leave, it would be to help her, and not, as it was in fact, to avoid my feelings.

'Hi Jenny', I said nervously, as if I had unconsciously inhabited her emotional state.

She looked up briefly, 'Hi'.

I explained my role and asked about previous social workers. She answered cautiously and politely, as if she was tasked with answering questions with the least number of words possible without being rude. I knew the police had been around the night before, and there had been lots of commotion between her parents and neighbours. Jenny had been observed by the police crying out for her mum to come back into the house as she held back her younger brothers from peering outside.

'How's life Jenny?' I asked, starting generally.

'It's okay, no, it's good, really good.'

'How did you spend your evening last night?' I asked.

Promptly, she replied, 'I don't know, not much, just watched television.'

'Jenny, I am aware the police came to your house last night – could you tell me what happened?'

She took a silent inhale and pulled a piece of skin off the side of her nail as if to manage the increased anxiety, 'I don't know.'

'You don't know?' I paraphrased.

'No', she said.

We sat in silence, before she said, 'Can I go back to class now, I think I got to be back now.'

'You are very welcome to go back to class, Jenny, although I did check with your teacher and she is absolutely fine with you being here. I can imagine it must be hard talking about what happened last night. Perhaps you are worried that you might get into trouble.'

She nodded, sniffed, and wiped her now moist eyes. I moved away from the topic and into more trivial and playful topics. She responded in kind, her body language softened, and she was relatively happy by the time the session ended.

Jenny couldn't speak to me about her experiences, and so I failed if that was the metric by which I judged my success as a social worker. However, in this instance, I felt confident that I had at least given Jenny the best chance to speak to me. Furthermore, Jenny's inability to share her thoughts and feelings about what would have been a frightening experience could be used as a way of obtaining her wishes and feelings.

At the very least, I could write in my report,

> Jenny doesn't feel able to share her thoughts and feelings, and as a result, she experienced what is likely a distressing altercation between her neighbours and parents, and she is left to deal with the thoughts and feelings without sharing them with anyone. Not able to share bad experiences might place Jenny under emotional strain, impacting on her well-being.

If appropriate, I could put forward a hypothesis around her reluctance to share her thoughts and feelings about this incident. For example, it is not uncommon for parents to tell their children not to speak to the social worker. I would, however, only include this in a report if it was clear that this was the case and it wasn't just speculation.

The second challenge is when children have developed strategies to cope with their experiences. The two reactions I have experienced the most reflect the Type A and Type C strategies. Children who use a Type A strategy cope with their experiences by ignoring or minimizing the effects of adverse events. They learn to inhibit and hide their emotions and comply with adults or try to take care of them in a role-reversing strategy. Part of their difficulty in opening up is that they have developed a self-protective coping mechanism that requires them to avoid negative feelings and, therefore, distract from topics that invoke negative feelings.

Conversely, children using a Type C strategy can be hyperactive, unable to concentrate and flit about from one task to another. They will refuse to join in with a conversation or a game designed to elicit their wishes and feelings through challenging, provocative behaviour. These children are anxious, and the distracted/distracting behaviour might function in a home where the problems are too threatening or scary for them to attend to but too important to entirely ignore. Therefore, they find engaging in a sustained dialogue challenging, especially about difficulties at home. This was the challenge I faced when attempting direct work with Charlie, whom I talked about in the previous chapter.

If these strategies dominate our sessions, I seek to find out whether the strategy I observe is consistent with observations of the children at home with their parents' and teachers' experiences of them. If so, I use this information to describe their behaviour and what I consider the function of this behaviour to be. To this effect, describing their coping strategies is a way of encapsulating their wishes and feelings.

Helping children understand their experiences

As well as learning how to elicit children's wishes and feelings, I had to learn how to communicate with children about issues they were exposed to in their life, such as domestic abuse, parental mental ill health and substance misuse.

I have worked with many parents who have experienced adverse life events growing up, such as their own parents separating, moving schools, the loss of a parent or brother or sister, or being placed into foster care without being provided with an explanation as to why. This can sometimes cause lasting and enduring effects, leaving them confused and distressed many years after the event.

I have also worked with many children who have a child protection plan or who have been removed from their parents' care and don't fully understand the reasons. There is a paradox in child protection in that the removal of a child is often done to protect the child, and yet it can be experienced by children as the most traumatic event of their life. Therefore, explanations for children and adults need to consider multiple perspectives.

I have concluded as a result of these experiences and reading the literature on trauma that helping children understand events in their lives is one of the most powerful interventions we can provide. Susie Essex is the principal co-creator of the resolutions approach. In a co-authored book with Andrew Turnell, *Working with Denied Child Abuse* (2006), they outline an innovative approach to working with denial. Part of this approach includes creating a 'Words and Pictures' explanation, an approach borne out of Susie's experience as a child protection chair, where many children didn't know the reason for social work involvement. Words and Pictures is a process where the professionals and parents work together to create an age-appropriate explanation for the children, telling them what children's services are worried about. It is focused on answering four questions:

1. Who is worried?
2. What are they worried about?
3. What happened?
4. What are people doing about it?

A vital element of this process is involving the parents. Parents are often apprehensive about their children knowing the reasons for our involvement, but once they understand the benefits for their child's understanding, they are, in my experience, relatively easily persuaded. I often explain that, without an explanation, children are prone to make up their own reasons, which can sometimes be worse in their imagination than the real reason. Also, young children are prone to ego-centric thinking, making them vulnerable to thinking that they are the reason for bad things happening and that something is wrong with them.

Helping children understand the reasons for our involvement will reduce self-blame and their anxiety. It can be a therapeutic intervention in itself. I explain that children who understand what has happened in their life, especially around key events that might have caused distress, tend to cope better than children who might have had the same experience but who have had no chance to talk about it, or feel they had to keep it to themselves.

Here are some examples I have used to help children understand what is happening:

Example 1: Mummy really loves you and has tried her hardest to look after you. Since you were a baby there have been worries about you and Mummy. This is because Mummy found it hard to look after you. When you were born Mummy was poorly with an illness called depression. Depression is an illness that makes people feel very sad for a long time, often for no reason. This meant that Mummy didn't sleep well, so she was very tired and didn't eat properly and felt weak. The doctor tried to give Mummy good medicine to help her feel better, but she didn't always take it like she should, so it didn't work.

Example 2: Sometimes Mummy would drink alcohol or take drugs. This affected her behaviour; she would stumble over, hurt herself or get upset and throw things. Mummy thought that if she drank alcohol or took drugs, she would feel better. At first, she did, but then she needed to keep taking them to feel better. After a while, she realized that she needed more and more, but because drugs are not good medicine like you get from the doctor, they eventually made her worse.

Example 3: Sometimes, Mummy and Daddy would shout and fight with each other. When young children see or hear grown-ups shouting and fighting, they can find this scary and upsetting. Sometimes, when Mummy and Daddy had fights, the police would come to check that everybody was okay. The police would ask Daddy to leave the home so that he could calm down.

Example 4: Richard, the social worker, was asked to write a report about Mummy and Daddy. The report was about how well Mummy and Daddy looked after you. At the end of the report, Richard wrote that he was very worried about you not being looked after properly by Mummy or Daddy. Richard asked a judge from a family court to read his report about Mummy and Daddy and asked the judge what to do next. A judge is a wise person, and it is their job to listen to Mummy, Daddy and Richard's worries, and decide the best thing to do for you. The judge decided that you should live with foster carers. Foster carers are special people who look after special children who can't live with their mummy or daddy.

I learned to write about these topics from reading other examples and referring to a brilliant book called *Adoption Conversations: How, When and What to Tell* by Renee Wolfs (2008), which provides explanations to give children for each issue, depending on their age.

Words and Pictures not only provided me with an invaluable tool to help children understand their experiences, but it also improved my confidence in undertaking direct work because I felt more comfortable exploring these issues.

Conclusion

Direct work with children is the most important, exhilarating, challenging, emotionally demanding and rewarding aspect of being a social worker. In this chapter, I have shared some ideas and tools that have supported me to undertake direct work with the children. Some of these might work for you; some, or many, may not.

In my experience, children and young people do not care what tool, method or approach we use. But they do care, in profound and often unspoken terms, about our intention, thoughtfulness and ability to show positive regard. Fundamentally, children need to know that we care about them. Deeply and personally. Perhaps that is the greatest gift we can offer children in our work with them, and who knows, it might even supersede any intervention we offer.

CHAPTER 4

Working with Parents

I ARRIVED AT JOAN AND JOHN'S HOME (Daniel's foster parents) to pick up Daniel, aged 16. As I approached their front door, I spotted Daniel clutching his luggage with an air of nonchalance. His demeanour exuded an innocent child-like quality that sharply contrasted with his foster parents' drained and sorrowful expressions.

Earlier that morning Joan had called to tell me about her attempt to rouse Daniel for school. In the midst of a heated argument, Daniel's frustration had erupted into a violent outburst. He had seized a chair and hurled it across his bedroom, narrowly missing Joan, who had taken refuge behind the door. The chaos then continued as Daniel flung various objects at the door, including a lampshade, a keyboard and various stationery items. His fury extended to upending his bed, culminating in a climactic act of self-destruction as he sent his newly acquired gaming console hurtling through the window, which shattered on the garden path below.

This was not the first time such a thing had happened. This was Daniel's fifth foster placement in two years. Before coming into care, Daniel had faced every harm imaginable, including witnessing the violent and shocking murder of his dad.

I liked Daniel. He was 16, but looked 11. Almost everyone who read about him on paper was surprised by how small and childlike he was in his appearance when they met him. In documents, he was described as 'dangerous', 'intimidating', 'violent and unpredictable', 'high risk' and other alarming terms. These produced a discrepancy between his actual presentation and the sorts of images that come to mind when reading those descriptions.

Daniel's life had been desperately sad, and picking him up that day, I felt a mix of frustration, disappointment and despair. I felt that the system had let him down, and that I was failing him. I couldn't see how I could ever make a positive difference for him, and wondered whether what I was doing was actually worse than what he had already been through at home.

Daniel said his goodbyes to Joan and John and hopped into the car. We began the two-hour journey to the short-term residential placement I had spent the previous few hours frantically searching for.

'Where am I going this time?' Daniel asked me.

I replied, 'We found you a home to stay in for a short while, where instead of foster parents, there will be many carers who take turns looking after you, and the other children who live there.'

Unphased by this, he asked, 'What's it called?'

I went blank.

For the life of me, I couldn't remember. I had just been pleased that I had found somewhere, so I had jotted down the address and shot out of the office.

'You don't know do you, Rich?'

Shit, how bad is this? 'Um, yeah, um, yeah I do, it's called, um... Care For All, it's called Care For All.'

His raised eyebrows relaxed, and I just about reassured him.

Daniel fiddled with every button in the car as we drove; he changed the radio stations several times and moved his seat back and forth to get comfortable. He rummaged through the glove box and found a book on the Disney film, *Frozen* (a book that my three-year-old daughter loved), which had a CD attached to the inside front cover that narrated the story. Daniel put the CD into the player, and then listened to the 15-minute story, following the words and pictures in the book. He did this again. And again.

At that point, I saw a young boy who needed desperately to be looked after, nurtured and offered care that would compensate for his earlier harmful experiences. Daniel was highly distrustful of others and highly sensitive to any form of rejection. It wasn't a case of if he would be rejected, but when.

Rather than wait, he seized control by seeking out what his experiences had taught him was inevitable. From his perspective, his behaviour was highly self-protective and a logical way of dealing with relationships. From his carers' perspective, they could see the vulnerability lurking behind his hard exterior and wanted to help him, but they found his unpredictable anger frightening and anxiety-provoking.

From a professional's perspective...well, that would depend on at what point a professional met Daniel in his life. If they had met him when he was eight years old, they would have seen a cheeky, likeable young boy, and frame his challenging behaviour as an understandable response to the traumatizing conditions he had been situated in. If they had met him when I did, they would perhaps still see his vulnerable side, but increasingly frame him as a dangerous young person with a profile that made professionals working with him feel despondent. In adulthood, especially if he were a parent, he would likely be seen as a 'perpetrator' and 'high risk'.

This chapter is about how we conceptualize parents' difficulties, and I began with Daniel, who was transitioning from adolescence to adulthood, to illustrate, in Crittenden's words, that 'today's parents' are 'yesterday's children' (2016, p.12). As Daniel moves into adulthood, he is undergoing changes, but even more significant, the way that professionals like me respond to him will also change.

If he becomes a parent, that shift might be even more stark. And yet, he will still be that little traumatized boy with unmet needs, albeit masked by a strategy in which he is able to conceal his vulnerability. Or rather, a strategy whereby he connivingly transforms his vulnerability into a tough exterior to protect himself, desperately trying to prevent himself from ever being hurt again.

I will also share in this chapter how I have come to learn that many issues we deal with in child protection, such as substance misuse, domestic abuse and mental ill health, are symptoms of an underlying issue that often has its roots in the parent's own childhood. I also

The Hatleys

Entering the Hatleys' home for the first time, I felt both over- and underwhelmed at the same time. Jackie had four children and was pregnant with her fifth. She told me about a series of partners she had had, and how each relationship had started off so positively. Tony, who she said was sweet and gentle, and occasionally liked a drink, turned out to be an alcoholic. She recalled, 'He hid empty bottles and cans everywhere and he thought I didn't know, I didn't say anything to him, but after I found Jolene trying to drink out of an empty can I found that was it, he was gone.' John had been extravagantly loving and had made her feel special before he turned controlling and occasionally violent. And Jake was addicted to cocaine and had racked up thousands of pounds in debt in her name. She just wanted to have a family of her own and had been repeatedly let down and disappointed by her partners' false promises. Billy and Ben were twins, aged five, Jolene was three and Jade was nine months old.

The living room had no carpet and the walls were painted black, and apart from a sofa and a television on a broken wooden stand that had been coloured in haphazardly by the children, the place was bare. There were three toys downstairs for the four children: a VTech Sit-to-Stand Learning Walker, a Fisher-Price baby bouncer, with the material faded and stained, and a large transporter truck, with no cars to transport.

As I walked upstairs, I smelt urine. Billy and Ben had bunk beds with blankets and pillows but no sheets or pillowcases. Jolene's worn-out and threadbare mattress, with springs poking out, was on the floor. Jade slept in a cot that was urine-soaked and wet from the night before.

'Oh, I was just about to change that actually, I just haven't stopped all day', Jackie said when she saw me looking at the cot.

There were several – mostly broken – toys scattered around the floor, mixed in with various items of clothing. Wardrobes were non-existent, but there was a set of drawers in the corner.

Every time I visited the family, Billy and Ben interacted with me with intensity – it was as if my visits were their first and last chance for human interaction. On the first occasion I met Jolene, she walked up to me with an irresistibly cute look, opened her arms and persistently signalled for me to pick her up. For a brief moment, I felt proud of my newly acquired communication skills, and silently patted myself on the back before Jackie said, 'She does that with everyone.' When I visited, she always craved physical affection from me, stroking, hitting or cuddling into me. Jade, the youngest, was often in her bouncer, looking vacant and sad, as if she had already given up on life.

We had made no progress in the previous six months of working with the family under a child in need plan and one year of working with Jackie under a child protection plan. Day after day, week after week, month after month, the home conditions remained depressingly the same.

During one visit, Jackie complained, 'You say the children are in the neglected category, but I do everything for them, make sure they're fed, clothed, and nothing I do is ever good enough for you is it? You just make me jump through hoops for the sake of it and it's destroying my mental health, making me always anxious.'

Despite her occasional moments of resistance, Jackie was mostly passive and compliant. To be fair to her, she did do everything – even when she didn't want to – but it just didn't seem to make a difference. Once, when Jackie and the children were infested with headlice, I de-nitted Jackie's hair and I taught her how to do the same with her children. I had mixed feelings doing this. I was grateful that she would allow me to undertake such a personal act, which cultivated a kind of intimacy between us. Although I felt disgusted at the grease and volume of nits coming out, I experienced some pleasure from being able to provide some practical, hands-on support, which was in sharp contrast to how I spent most of my time as a social worker.

Other professionals were extremely concerned about the children, and frequently vented their frustration about the lack of change. I understood their frustrations, and tried to relay this to my manager, but she would say, 'Rich, we need to demonstrate we've done everything we can to help Jackie.' She would then make suggestions for a different type of support we hadn't tried. I didn't really understand my manager's position because the children were suffering – all four were significantly delayed in various ways, so why couldn't we seek removal? Surely foster care would solve all these problems?

I also felt frustrated and would alternate between feeling sorry for Jackie and angry about what she was doing to her children. When she blamed me for ruining her mental health, I would feel even more angry. I also felt like a failure and unable to make her change. At least seeking removal would make me feel like I was doing something. It would also stop me from waking up in the middle of the night, fraught with anxiety and fear about the children's safety, questioning whether I was doing enough.

Eventually, we did enter into pre-proceedings. As part of this process, I did a parenting assessment. Even though I had worked with the family for 18 months, I had never had the chance to sit for a few hours and really get to know Jackie. In the office, I printed off the Adult Attachment Interview I found online and asked Jackie the questions.

Jackie told me that her mum had had her when she was 17, when she was in an extremely violent relationship with her father, aged 27. He was a notorious drug dealer. Her parents separated when she was 18 months old following a violent assault that resulted in her father's imprisonment. Her father was in and out of prison throughout Jackie's childhood and took little interest in her. Aged seven, Jackie came home from school to find her mum unconscious on the living room floor, surrounded by needles and empty beer bottles. After two weeks in a coma, Jackie's mum died. Jackie then went to live with her aunt, who had multiple sclerosis and limited mobility.

Jackie said,

When I was with my aunt, it was like a bunch of feelings hitting me hard. I was angry, sad, confused and just all mixed up 'cause I didn't get why suddenly it all...one day, it's just going to school like normal, and then next thing, mum's gone, and off to live with my aunt. What? Wait, who? What? Why? Where? It was too much and, so, umm, didn't talk much to anyone back then. I kinda messed up, started with the drinks and drugs, went off the rails, it's all my fault no one to blame but me, didn't talk to nobody, just went with it, bottled everything. Sometimes, you just shove the bad stuff away in your head and your brain sorta forgets what you want it to forget, just blanks it out, blanks out all the bad stuff.

Jackie said that she absolutely adored her aunt and that she was the only one who was ever really there for her, but she also recalled how she had needed to care for her aunt when her health went massively downhill when Jackie was a teenager. She looked after her aunt until she died, when Jackie was 15. Jackie stopped attending school when she was 12 years old because 'I was so sick of being bullied, telling the teachers and nothing happening', and began drinking daily from the age of 13: 'It helped me forget everything, and I had nothing to live for, so why not, I didn't care about myself or anything.'

Aged 17, like her mum, she fell pregnant with her boyfriend whom she had known since she was nine. He killed himself when she was seven months pregnant. Jackie said, 'When I knew I was pregnant, I never touched a drop of alcohol again. I seen what it did to my mum and never wanted my kids to have that.'

It was heartbreaking. And desperately sad.

Three months after this interview, we issued care proceedings. Billy, Ben, Jolene and Jade were placed in two foster placements. Billy and Ben then remained in foster care while Jolene and Jade were adopted. When Jackie gave birth to her fifth child alone, he was also removed and placed for adoption.

Exhausting all options

Over the years, I have learned several lessons from working with parents like Jackie. Although it was frustrating at the time, I was so grateful that my manager had ensured that we had done everything possible to try to support Jackie. At the conclusion of the care proceedings, I didn't gain much satisfaction from the courts endorsing my recommendation that the children be removed and placed in alternative care despite all the work that had gone into achieving that outcome. I trusted it was the right decision for the children, yet I felt deflated and underwhelmed.

I left the courtroom thinking that perhaps we (a collective 'we', as a society and children's social care) had failed Jackie as a child. Jackie had had her self-esteem, self-worth, ability to trust in others and, ultimately, her entire childhood violently taken away from her through her upbringing. Her experiences had left her with limited coping skills and unable to care for her own children. Not only had Jackie's own parents taken away her childhood, they had also taken away her opportunity to care for her own children (and, no doubt, going back a generation, I would have found a similar tale for Jackie's parents).

Confusingly for Jackie, she was providing her children with a better standard of care than she had received, yet here we were. A key consolation I could hold on to, however, was confidence that we had done everything possible to support Jackie within the context of the support that was available. I have learned that it is not enough to demonstrate that children are suffering significant harm, but that they are suffering significant, enduring harm and that we have done everything possible to support their parent(s) over a prolonged period.

Adversity and addiction

In working with Jackie and many other parents, I increasingly began to see a link between childhood adversity and trauma and substance misuse. Drugs and alcohol helped Jackie cope with an intolerable past. They were a solution. And a highly effective one at that in helping her deal with the unbearable distress associated with the loss, abandonment and deep-rooted feelings of shame that stemmed from such experiences in her childhood.

Gabor Maté, in *The Realm of Hungry Ghosts*, writes that substance misuse 'originates in a human being's desperate attempt to solve a problem' and 'the problem of emotional pain, of overwhelming stress, of lost connection, of loss of control, of a deep discomfort with the self. In short, it is a forlorn attempt to solve the problem of human pain'. Therefore, when working with those experiencing addiction issues, his mantra has become: 'The first question is not "Why the addiction", but "Why the pain?"' (2018, p.xix).

Drugs and alcohol are effective because they artificially create satisfying emotional states that typically derive from being well connected to others. Or because they numb the psychological distress caused by fractured or abusive relationships. This is a very different way of thinking about people with an addiction to the common portrayal that they are making a choice in pursuit of hedonism or pleasure.

Therefore, merely asking a parent to stop, or pointing out that by taking drugs and alcohol they are harming their children, is unlikely to work, even when the stakes are high. 'To expect an addict to give up her drug', Maté writes, 'is like asking the average person to imagine living without all her social skills, support networks, emotional stability, and sense of physical and psychological comfort. Those are the qualities that, in their illusory and evanescent way, drugs give the addict' (2018, p.305).

Jackie had managed to abstain from drugs and alcohol once she found out she was pregnant, which was all the more impressive given that she did it without help and during a time when her partner had died by suicide. She would have likely experienced withdrawals, and in the absence of pain-blocking substances, I suspect she would have been confronted with distressing thoughts and feelings tied to her past and current experiences.

Nevertheless, her determination to provide her child with a different life from the one she herself had had meant she persevered. It's hard to deny the courage and fortitude she showed. I must admit, though, that I struggled to hold on to this when working with her. The level of care she provided to her children was woefully inadequate, but like nearly all the parents I worked with, it wasn't through lack of trying or due to a lack of love for her children.

Treating the symptom rather than the cause

After a few years, I realized that in my work helping parents, I was often caught up in addressing the symptom rather than the cause. With Jackie, for example, she had attended parenting programmes to improve her knowledge (she had attended Incredible Years three times), parent–child interventions to help her relationship with her child (Theraplay), and a one-to-one family support who helped her with routines and setting boundaries – and made applications to charities for furniture and the Freedom Programme to identify and avoid abusive relationships. It was only after I listened to Jackie's experiences during the Adult Attachment Interview that I realized that these support services – repeated on rotation – weren't going to make a difference. On reflection, perhaps this was obvious because the concerns remained unchanged despite her engaging with the support.

More than that, though, it was increasingly evident to me that Jackie's profound difficulties with parenting were tied to her childhood experiences. In the absence of being supported to work through those, I began to see that change was unlikely to occur. In other words, we were treating the symptoms of an underlying problem under the mistaken belief that the symptoms were the problem.

A framework for understanding neglect

It wasn't until I read a paper by Crittenden, titled 'An information processing perspective on the behavior of neglectful parents' (1993) that I would come close to understanding why Jackie couldn't benefit from the support we had offered her. Crittenden identified four stages at which parents could fail to meet their child's needs. She put forward the theory that for a parent to respond to a child's needs sensitively, the parent has to: (1) perceive the child's need; (2) accurately interpret the need; (3) select a response; (4) implement a response.

At each step, there is the risk that something may go wrong. At the first step, a parent could fail to perceive their child's needs and signals – severe depression or substance misuse may contribute to a parent not noticing the child's signal of need. At the second step, the parent might pick up on the child's need, but misinterpret the meaning. Some parents, for example, think that their child is trying to personally attack them, even when they are infants and obviously incapable of feeling that way at that age. Alternatively, a parent might believe that their baby is fussy or needy, so they react in a way that dismisses their needs.

At the third step, the parent might perceive and interpret the child's needs accurately, but select the wrong response. Finally, at the fourth stage, the parent might not implement the response or get delayed because of other pressures in the family. In families with many problems and lots of children, a parent might know what their child needs and how to respond, but get distracted or pulled away by some other crisis. Or the parent's own needs take precedence.

The support we offered Jackie had been focused on step 2, helping her interpret her child's needs (with parent–child therapy), and steps 3 and 4, selecting and implementing a response (with parenting programmes). I realized these interventions couldn't work because Jackie often didn't perceive her children's needs (step 1). During one visit, Jolene had approached her, holding out an empty beaker, signalling she wanted to a drink. This didn't register for Jackie. After several failed attempts, Jolene wandered off and threw her empty beaker across the room a minute later. At that point, Jackie noticed the negative behaviour, did what she had been taught, and placed Jolene on the naughty step. Jolene never got a drink.

In exploring Jackie's history through the Adult Attachment Interview, it became apparent that in the context of uniformly disappointing relationships, whereby she was repeatedly hurt in her intimate relationships, she had shut herself down emotionally. This kept the heartache, rejection and feelings of worthlessness at a distance. Although self-protective, learning to disconnect from her feelings meant she could not perceive her children's needs, which were communicated to her through the display of their feelings. This also impacted her adult relationships because she had learned that she was worthy of mistreatment, unlovable and, ultimately, unable to influence her circumstances.

Recognizing this doesn't, of course, change the children's lived experience in her care. However, providing a context to understand her difficulties allows for a more compassionate stance. A report that accurately captured her difficulties might help Billy, Ben, Jolene and Jade understand that it wasn't that their mother didn't love them or because they were not good or loveable enough; rather, that she had severely challenging circumstances that rendered her unable to offer the care they needed.

Furthermore, and crucially, such an understanding would provide clues as to what might help Jackie, such as intensive psychotherapeutic support to help her make sense of her childhood experiences. Or a transitional attachment figure who could offer her the care she wanted to provide her children with, someone who could work alongside her long term, like a grandparent figure. If Jackie could feel looked after, nurtured and held, then she might, in turn, be able to provide this for her children.

Conclusion

I began this chapter with Daniel, a young man entering adulthood with a set of coping strategies that made him insecure, anxious and prone towards aggression and violence. Recognizing the underlying nature of his difficulties might go some way to developing a more compassionate view towards him, but if his behaviour begins to affect a vulnerable child, our focus, understandably, will inevitably turn towards the child. This was the case when working with Jackie, whose coping strategies didn't result in her being violent, but rather disconnected, passive and helpless.

'Compassion is an elusive concept', Crittenden writes. It 'depends upon full awareness of both the experiences of each individual and their potential for growth and change...one can, like a good parent, hold all the needs and perspectives in mind' (2016, p.291).

This requires that we hold on to the fact that parents who harm their children often don't intend to, yet their children still need to be safeguarded, whatever the underlying reason. This is no easy feat. Empathy for a parent's behaviour, especially when it harms a child, can feel like we are accepting or condoning it, perhaps at the expense of the child. And our ability to empathize can be challenged when we work with parents who display hostile and aggressive behaviour.

Indeed, understanding the underlying nature of parents' difficulties does not, unfortunately, inculcate us from the interpersonal effects of being shouted at, abused, provoked or threatened, which occur all too often in our work. Exploring how we work with parents where there is denial, resistance or conflict is the subject of the next chapter.

CHAPTER 5

Working Directly with Parents

IN THIS CHAPTER, I argue that the role of a child protection social worker is inherently conflict-ridden. The main reason for this is that we often work with parents who don't want to work with us. In children's services we, as professionals, start the relationship and most often dictate when the relationship ends. It's an involuntary relationship, and I don't think as a profession we have been good at theorizing and framing how to build collaboration with people who don't want us in their lives (with the exception of Ferguson 2011 and Forrester *et al.* 2019). Parents often have little confidence that we can be of benefit to them.

If my job were to help a family in need who wanted it, that would be pretty straightforward. Instead, my job is to decide whether a parent needs support, and whether it's necessary to impose that support against their will in the pursuit of safeguarding their child.

The inevitability of conflict

When deciding whether to curtail a parent's freedom and liberty, the role is often about managing the complex dynamics produced as a result. Here are some examples of conflict stemming from this:

- When I needed to visit Charlie, a child subject to a child protection plan, his mum told me that she didn't want me to see him and that he was scared of meeting new people.

- When I spoke to Frankie about the impact her suspected drug use was having on her unborn baby, she adamantly denied drug use.
- When I had to write a conference report about home conditions being unhygienic and unsafe, Jackie was affronted and vehemently disagreed.
- When I had to deliver a pre-proceedings letter to Matt and Helen, Helen ripped the letter up on the doorstep, screamed at me to 'fuck off' and called me a 'cunt'.

In each of these examples, the parents were reacting to a power imbalance and a sense of injustice, where, from their perspective, they were having their right to a private family life taken away. Many parents' dissatisfaction expressed towards me was because of what I represented: a statutory organization. They didn't want me involved, not necessarily because of who I was, but because of what I represented.

There are at least two reasons for this. First, there is often a disagreement about the legitimacy of the concerns identified about the child (which we will explore later in this chapter). Second, most parents fear that social work involvement could result in the loss of their child. It's hard to imagine many people would want to work with a system where that could be the outcome, even if it meant access to some much-needed help.

Lady Hale, a retired judge, captured this in a speech she made 30 years after the inception of the Children Act 1989, an act which she led the creation of: 'the aspiration of developing a partnership between children's services and families with children in need proved very difficult to achieve... The trouble is that, if efforts to work with families run into difficulties, the local authority can always resort to care proceedings and the families know that' (2019, p.11).

Therefore, a central task in child protection is learning to manage conflict, which requires us to recognize the power bestowed on us as statutory social workers. This was difficult for me to acknowledge at first. I was too caught up in my own fear, anxiety and constant self-evaluation of whether I was saying or doing the right thing. For example, when I went to my first child protection case conference, it felt like a significant moment in my career. I was excited about doing something new, yet I was nervous and unsure of myself. Consumed by intense feelings, I didn't contemplate the range of possible feelings the parents might experience entering an unfamiliar, formal room, a room full of unfamiliar professionals using formal language to discuss the most intimate and potentially shameful aspects of their lives.

The imbalance of power and parents' fear of social work involvement also made it hard to build a collaborative working relationship. One way this manifested was that there would be different views on what the problem was, and when I remained fixated on being 'right', the relationship would run into trouble.

On one occasion we received information that Louise, a mum we were working with, had been observed intoxicated with her three young children. The social worker was on leave, so a senior social worker and I went out to visit Louise mid-morning. My colleague, Carol, was an older, much more experienced social worker who had previously worked in some of the toughest and most deprived communities in England. I felt like she could handle anything. On the other hand, I was fresh out of university.

After a few minutes of knocking on the door, peering round the side and into the letterbox, Louise opened the door, clearly drunk. The house we walked into was in disarray. Louise's son, Jack, six months old, was slumped in his buggy with the straps on, fast asleep. He looked like he had slept there all night. Lily-Mae, her older daughter, six years old, who was supposed to be in school, was upstairs. I went and spoke to Lily-Mae while Carol stayed with Louise.

Lily-Mae was sat on a bean bag in the corner of her room, with her headphones on, playing her games console. She was open and easy to connect with. She told me, 'Mummy had a party last night, and I couldn't sleep, I don't mind though, I can block it out with my headphones.'

I went downstairs and sat with Louise and Carol, who was asking Louise about her family, and she said, 'I don't have any family, all my family do is give me shit, never helped me.' Carol demonstrated lots of empathy to Louise and asked about her neighbours, tentatively mooting the idea that the children might need to be looked after by someone else for the time being.

'I am not even drunk', Louise slurred. I thought 'she clearly is', and felt compelled to intervene. I said, 'Lily-Mae said you had a party last night, how much did you drink?'

She replied, agitated, 'I told you, I, I, I haven't drunk anything, well, I had five cans last night and that's it.' 'There is no way she only had five cans', I thought to myself; she was lying. 'I think you have probably had more than five cans. How much have you really had?'

Louise started crying, and quickly turned agitated, and started shouting, 'Why are you saying I am lying? I only had five cans. I had a few drinks with my friends last night. Am I not allowed to have one night to myself?' My only thought was that before we could do anything else, she needed to admit her alcohol consumption.

Carol stepped in, 'It doesn't matter how much you drank. Look, Louise, we can see that you are really upset. It looks like it's a really tough time for you at the moment and so we would like to arrange for Jack and Lily-Mae to be looked after by someone you trust just so you can get the rest and recuperation you need. Can you help us with that?'

I had very few skills in responding to and managing parents when they had a different view to the problem. If a parent was dishonest, I would take this personally, as if they were trying to deceive me. In one way, I felt that Louise was trying to deceive me. But it is more accurate to say that she was trying to deceive a social worker, and I was the one standing in front of her that day. In other words, it wasn't personal. In responding to Louise lying to me personally, I had overlooked the power imbalance she was reacting to.

I was a young white male in a position of authority casting judgement on an economically deprived single mother struggling to live her life while raising two children. I was also contributing to an irresolvable dispute about the truth as if, in the absence of concrete, verifiable truth, we couldn't proceed. If a parent doesn't admit the whole truth, then they would never be able to address the issue. From this perspective, helping (or trying to make) a parent see the truth was a critical part of my role, I believed, because that was the precursor to being able to do anything about it. However, my colleague Carol proved that to be wrong. She didn't pursue the absolute truth and could still collaborate with Louise to achieve safety for her children.

How did she accomplish this? First, she didn't judge Louise for her predicament, which meant that Louise was less defensive towards her. Second, she focused on what needed to happen for the children to be safely cared for. In this instance, it was a short-term measure, but the same principle applies to longer-term issues. Third, Carol demonstrated a capacity to show empathy for Louise while simultaneously holding in mind the children's needs and her role in protecting those. She didn't fall into the trap of thinking empathy for Louise meant she condoned her behaviour or would cause her to overlook the children's needs; she could hold on to both perspectives.

Carol demonstrated what Forrester and his colleagues describe as the highest level of skill in communicating with parents in their paper called 'Communication skills in child protection: How do social workers talk to parents?' (2007). At the first level, we want to help parents. Social workers can feel uncomfortable with the power bestowed on them in their role, and consider it antithetical to their values. Therefore, they focus on helping and trying to negate the power dynamics. However, when the social worker has to exert authority and exercise their statutory duty, the relationship can turn fraught. When this happens, the parent can feel betrayed as they were unaware that this was a possible outcome in the context of the relationship. In some cases, a social worker might avoid implementing a statutory process for fear of upsetting their relationship with a parent, which involves overlooking the child's needs and right to protection.

At the second level, a social worker focuses exclusively on the child. This can help social workers avoid collusion with a parent, which can happen easily at the first level. But focusing on the child can often result in judgement and criticism. Getting caught in denial disputes and telling parents straight and forthrightly their wrongdoings is justified as a means of advocating on behalf of a child. While technically fulfilling the role of a child protection social worker, this is a very unhelpful, and ultimately counterproductive, way to build a collaborative relationship with a parent.

At the third and highest level, the social worker recognizes that they are working with a vulnerable adult as well as a vulnerable child. While a social worker might need to raise concerns and explain what that means regarding processes, this can be done with empathy, tact and respect.

Working with situational denial

I found practising within this third level easier once I understood the rationale behind why a parent might be dishonest. Returning to the work of Andrew Turnell and Susie Essex, they point out that there are 'many strong social and interactional pressures that make denial a compelling response' (2006, p.29). Many parents are highly fearful of social work intervention, and may overestimate the powers available to social workers, causing them to believe that their children can easily be removed. In other cases, where the children are subject to a child protection plan or pre-proceedings, the potential for care proceedings and thus the loss of their child is a real possibility.

In both instances, the families can easily conclude that sharing concerns or requesting help will be used unfavourably against them. This can result in disputes whereby the parents vehemently deny or minimize the issues at hand, and social workers can find themselves spending a lot of time trying to prove and demonstrate how a parent is incorrect.

Turnell and Essex point out that 'admission becomes the only portal by which safety can be achieved, and when the parents maintain a position of "denial" the professional imagination about what to do becomes exhausted' (2006, p.8). Once I understood this, I took a parent's dishonesty less personally and was able to convey empathy. It's not uncommon now for me to say something like,

I imagine that you are quite scared about sharing the extent of your alcohol problem because you are worried that it might mean that we will try to remove your child. That is a quite a common fear. Ultimately, it's up to you whether you decide to share with me, but in my experience, parents who don't share can't access the help that might support them change, the problems gets worse and then the risk we have to get involved at a more serious level increases.

I then explain the current process and possible outcomes if the situation doesn't change.

Working with psychological denial

As I took my seat in the hushed courtroom, a wave of anxiety washed over me. The room had no windows, but soft lighting cast a warm glow on the polished wood panelling. I sat adjacent to an elevated platform, which housed a wide bench the judge would sit behind. A Royal coat of arms emblem was majestically displayed in the middle of this large platform.

That morning, I had visited a family on a council estate in one of the most deprived communities in England. Now, I was wearing a full navy-blue suit in a sophisticated court building, with its neoclassical and modern architecture giving it a sense of grandeur. The contrast was disconcerting.

I sat with my manager to my left and the parents and grandparents to my right. The solicitors all sat in the row in front, symbolizing the hierarchy, with the most important players seated closest to the front. We sat in silence, awaiting the judge's entrance. The quietness allowed for a rare moment of peaceful reflection, and my mind wandered to what the others must be thinking.

I peered to my right, and the parents, Mike and Frankie, aged 17 and 19 respectively, were holding hands, grasping each other tightly and offering physical reassurance. Their sadness and pain quietly exuded from them, breaking through occasionally with Frankie sniffling. This was a brutal reality, and a surge of shame coursed through my whole body, causing me to shiver. The weight of my involvement within the system passed through momentarily.

Physiologically, Frankie was primed to look after Ava. After nine months of increasing discomfort, pain and anticipation, Frankie had given birth. Suddenly, all that pain dissipated and was replaced with intense and overwhelming love for the little, vulnerable, wide-eyed baby girl held in her arms. However, in this case, the opportunity to reap the reward of caring for Ava would be denied to her (at least in the short term). Frankie's body would nevertheless continue to release chemicals that sent signals to the brain to promote connection, attunement and attachment. Indeed, as we sat there waiting for the judge to arrive, Frankie rocked herself in a way that I imagined would help soothe Ava, their four-day-old baby, if she were in her arms.

Following the court hearing, I picked up Ava from the hospital and took her to her foster carers. The next day I supervised contact between Ava, Mike and Frankie. There was nothing distinctly concerning about their interactions; in fact, quite the opposite. They were loving, attentive and doting parents. Despite an adversarial relationship, and Mike and Frankie's dissatisfaction with social work involvement, I had a positive relationship with them, and we seemed to get along with one another. At times, we even laughed together.

A few weeks later, Mike and Frankie moved into a residential placement with Ava. Sadly, this didn't last. When Frankie arrived at the residential placement, she tested positive for a range of substances that she had denied using throughout her pregnancy. She had rejected the repeated concerns that had been raised about her drug use when I asked her during her pregnancy. Although abstinence was a precondition for the placement, they made an unusual allowance. A week later, Frankie went out with Ava, and then she went missing for 29 hours. She was eventually found by the police in what they described as a 'well-known crack den'. Frankie 'resisted arrest, kicking, screaming and spitting at the officers'.

The placement felt unable to continue supporting Frankie. I had known Frankie for a few months, and she was always polite and engaging, but her eyes gave away a sense of desperate, unresolved pain and suffering – it was etched into her body. I liked Frankie, and part of me felt that she needed another chance – she needed picking up, dusting down and encouraged to start again. Yet at the same time, I thought about Ava and the impact of spending nearly a day in a dark flat that was described as 'filthy, empty cans everywhere, smashed bottles, needles, and foil and other paraphernalia on the coffee table'. Mike stayed in the placement with Ava, and Frankie took the bus home. It must have been gut-wrenching for her to take the bus home without the two people she loved the most. I suspect she drank herself into oblivion.

I know I would.

In working with parents like Frankie and Mike, I was confronted with the reality that I couldn't make parents change, no matter how much I wanted to. Frankie had lied about her substance misuse during the several months I had worked with her before Ava was born, despite my attempt to empathize with the fear she might have about the consequence of social work involvement. Each and every time I presented her with a new concern – like a neighbour witnessing her drunk, the police suspecting she was intoxicated during an altercation with Mike or the reports from her family (who wanted to remain anonymous) about her drug use – she would minimize or deny the reports.

In his 2018 TEDx Talk, titled 'The gift of desperation', social worker and recovering addict Ian Thomas described denial as 'a psychological coping strategy designed to keep us emotionally stable in unstable times'. Another recovering addict turned neuroscientist and author, Marc Lewis, writes in *Memoirs of an Addicted Brain* that addiction is 'an attempted shortcut to get more of what you need by condensing "what you need" into a single monolithic, symbol. The drug (or other substance) stands for a cluster of needs...needs for warmth, safety, freedom, and self-sufficiency. Then it becomes too valuable, and you cannot live without it' (2011, p.305).

For Frankie and the many other parents I have worked with, they are profoundly fearful of losing access to and giving up a behaviour that helps them cope and deal with their emotional distress. It isn't simply a case of giving up a drug; it is giving up the only solution they have found to dealing with the unbearable psychological distress associated with their experiences, and trusting that their vulnerability, hurt and pain will be appropriately and sensitively handled through the relationships with others around them. Hardly an easy task. Especially given that relationships were the original source of their suffering.

I also learned that my ability to act as someone who could form a therapeutic alliance with a parent and cultivate a relationship that would be the catalyst for change was severely compromised. This was a disappointing realization, and my wish for it not to be the case meant I held onto the idea longer than I should have. This idea affected my self-efficacy because I would assume disproportionate responsibility when I was unable to afford it.

The challenge of forming a therapeutic alliance stemmed from the inherently conflictual nature of my role and power imbalance, which I have already discussed, but also because I simply didn't have the time to spend with parents to help them through the change process. Generally, I visited parents once a fortnight, once a week at most. And during these visits I would have other actions to take, such as seeing the bedrooms and speaking to the children. Therefore, I was often deprived of the two critical ingredients of a therapeutic relationship, psychological safety and time.

Unable to make parents change, and limited in my ability to function as a therapist, I found my role taking a different shape from the one I had initially imagined – albeit, and critically, a role that was no less significant or profound regarding my potential to make a difference. Fundamentally, my role, interpersonally at least, was to maximize the chance parents would change, while also explaining to them the consequences should change not occur, as that was the most effective way to reduce the harm their behaviour had on their children. I had to establish a clearer concept of a working relationship, which functioned to serve a purpose of getting the job done.

The aim of my involvement was to reduce the concerns held for the children, so they weren't exposed to significant harm. An important distinction to make here is that it is *not* the role of a social worker to make children safe. That is an unattainable goal, and one that if I aspired to achieve it would leave me perpetually dissatisfied. Reducing harm was the goal, not eradicating it.

This point was made by Mr Judge Hedley, in the now famously held case law *Re L*:[1]

> ...society must be willing to tolerate very diverse standards of parenting, including the eccentric, the barely adequate and the inconsistent. It follows too that children will inevitably have both very different experiences of parenting and very unequal consequences flowing from it. It means that some children will experience disadvantage and harm, while others will flourish in atmospheres of loving security and emotional stability. These are the consequences of our fallible humanity, and it is not the provenance of the state to spare children all the consequences of defective parenting. In any event, it simply could not be done.

Principles for effective child protection practice

In pursuit of helping parents improve their children's situation, and considering the lessons explored above, I found that my role was to form a working relationship – ideally one that was collaborative – so that the task of helping and protecting children could be achieved.

Here are five key principles that helped with this endeavour.

1. Valuing parents

The most effective way to help children is to help their parents. This requires a delicate balance of finding ways to build a relationship while also having difficult conversations about change and what statutory process will be followed in the absence of change.

---

1   *Re L (Care: Threshold Criteria) [2007] EWHC 447 (Fam) (Hedley J).*

After a few years of practice, I encountered similar themes and issues. When I started to think, 'this is another DV [domestic violence] case' or 'this is just another substance misuse case', I knew I was losing the individuality and humanity of the person, overlooking what was unique about that person. Because of the focus in child protection on protecting the child, it can be easy to overlook parents as people, and instead focus on them purely in terms of their risk to children.

As a result of finding myself falling into this trap of viewing parents as an amalgamation of risk factors, I tried to build relationships with them, and learn about them and the type of person they were. What were their interests and hobbies? What type of life did they want to live? What aspirations and goals did they have?

2. Finding common ground

One of the most important and transformative ideas for my practice with parents I learned was from Signs of Safety, and this was identifying overlapping goals between parents and myself. As pointed out by social workers Andrew Turnell and Steve Edwards, in their original book *Signs of Safety*, 'Often, service recipients are not willing to change simply to satisfy society's (or the government's) standards, but will be motivated by their own goal of avoiding (what they see as) outside interference in their family' (1999, p.69).

Asking parents 'What do you want to happen?' almost without fail elicits the response, 'We don't want a social worker in our life'. I can acknowledge this and demonstrate empathy, recognizing that their dissatisfaction isn't about me, but about what I represent. Following this, I share with them that I have a similar goal: 'Social workers don't want to be involved unless we must, so how can we work together to show that social care doesn't need to be involved?'

There are two additional elements to this. First, I learned to demonstrate empathy both for their fear of social work involvement and for the difficulties they were experiencing. In relation to hearing their fear and apprehension about social work involvement, I found it was essential not to get caught up in retorting explanations or justifications immediately. I could acknowledge their feelings, even if I didn't necessarily agree with them. Often, but not always, this approach reduces the parent's defensiveness and creates openness to discuss their difficulties. This revealed to me how defensiveness isn't a trait that a parent has or doesn't have, but instead is created within the context of a relationship.

Concerning their difficulties (substance misuse, domestic abuse, etc.), I was keen to show genuine curiosity about the reason for the parent's difficulty, working from the assumption that it must help them in some way (even if it has a significant cost). As pointed out by Maté (2018, p.33), 'It is impossible to understand addiction without asking what relief the addict finds, or hopes to find, in the drug or the addictive behaviour'.

We can replace the word 'addiction' with any other type of behaviour; in fact, many of the behaviours we encounter in child protection could be conceptualized as addictions (behavioural, psychological and interpersonal).

3. Holding on to multiple perspectives

In the case of a father addicted to alcohol and disposed towards hostility and aggression, this would involve (1) compassion towards the father's behaviour, attempting to appreciate that his anger might be motivated by a profound fear of needing to change or losing his child (a parent can be both frightened and frightening); (2) recognition of the harm experienced by the child being cared for by a father dependent on alcohol and behaving aggressively towards a social worker; and (3) acknowledging the feelings experienced due to the father's aggressive behaviour on the self, and using appropriate outlets to share emotions, such as supervision, so as not to allow them to influence the relationship negatively.

4. (Re)defining what constitutes a good outcome

Figuring out what constitutes a good outcome in child protection is complicated. But it is important to do. Outcomes can be defined in two ways. First is in the obvious sense of what the outcome is (e.g., the child on the child protection plan, the child subject to a Supervision Order, etc.). The challenge of this is immediately apparent when you think about the removal of a child. On the face of it, it isn't a good outcome. But it might be the best outcome for that child, depending on their situation. To complicate matters further, different people will have different perspectives on the same outcome.

A parent is likely to be devastated, traumatized and angry that their child has, from their perspective, been unjustly removed from their care. Conversely, the child might be relieved and grateful for the chance to be safely cared for. Alternatively, they could be deeply unhappy about being removed, but both their parents' feelings and their own distress wouldn't necessarily mean it was a bad outcome.

Therefore, outcomes in child protection need to be thought through carefully and, in my opinion, based on the process through which an outcome is achieved rather than what the outcome is. Applying this relationally, a good outcome for me would be whether I felt I could convey empathy, facilitate the parent's ability to think about change, and clearly explain the processes of ongoing statutory involvement. In this sense, it would be about whether I had upheld the parent's rights in an ethical and judicious manner.

In reflecting on Frankie and Mike, I felt I demonstrated these attributes, even though it didn't bring about the change I hoped for. Regarding outcomes for Ava, she needed to be given every chance to be looked after by her parents. A critical ingredient of this was ensuring that Frankie and Mike were given the very best chance of engaging in the support that would help them make the necessary changes. I believe they were provided with this through a residential placement that provided high support and therapeutic input. Unfortunately, Frankie wasn't in a place in her life where she would use this to her benefit. Mike, however, was able to remain looking after his daughter, and when care proceedings ended, he was looking after her in the community successfully.

5. Facilitating talk about change and consequences

Although I have outlined the limitations I experienced in building therapeutic and reciprocal relationships with parents within a child protection context, I nevertheless believe that our role and relational skills are of paramount importance. A critical element of this is helping parents see some of the benefits that could be derived from changing, and then functioning as a bridge between where they are and where they want to be and the support services that will enable them to take on that journey. This is very different from telling parents what they need to change, how they need to change, and then making expectations for them to engage in the support services we've identified.

There are three steps to this: understanding behaviour; asking about self-identified goals; and explaining consequences. Seeking to understand how the behaviour helps them, either currently or in the past, is first. Most behaviour, even behaviour that seems illogical, self-destructive or harmful to others, has an underlying self-protective function. Connecting with this underlying reason requires curiosity and empathy. To be done effectively, it requires we dispense with all judgement, even if only momentarily, to discover how this behaviour has served them.

Second is asking them whether they want to do anything about the behaviour, and if they did, what they would imagine to be the benefits if they could. Almost any behaviour, even harmful behaviour, often has both advantages and disadvantages. So it is common for parents to alternate between giving reasons for and against change. As social workers are under pressure to bring about change, the risk here is that we jump in to list all the reasons why they need to change, including adding to the list of disadvantages they haven't considered. This is a trap because, in my experience, it automatically makes parents more defensive and they close down.

Therefore, I try to focus on their desire to change and help them think about some of the advantages of them changing, and then link their self-identified desires with services that might support them with their journey.[2] We can't make people change, but we can help them think about their goals and identify the support that will help them.

Third, this conversation is then nested within broader conversations about consequences, which are framed in a particular way: first, it is not a punishment, but rather an explanation of consequences; and second, it is framed as a choice. It might be a very limited choice with few options, but it is a choice, nonetheless.

Conclusion

Building a relationship with parents in a child protection context is tough, emotionally taxing and intellectually challenging. Yet it can be profoundly rewarding and enjoyable, and a privilege. It requires courage, humility and tenacity.

A key element underpinning any approach is identifying personal values – what type of social worker would you want knocking on your door if you were traumatized, exhausted, struggling with addiction or in a violent relationship? If you reacted with fear, anger or avoidance, how would you want a social worker to treat you?

Building relationships in child protection requires identifying values we want to uphold, irrespective of the conditions (I explore this more in Chapter 8). Crittenden writes,

> Can we respond with mercy – even grace – when faced with the harm that some parents create? Can we acknowledge ignorance when we don't understand and don't know what to do, particularly when we don't understand the terrible tragedies humans impose on each other? Can we comfort those who have destroyed their world and that of others, even when we don't understand and even while we protect them from themselves? (2016, p.12)

---

2   Motivational interviewing provides excellent ideas and tools to navigate these conversations about change successfully. See *Motivational Interviewing for Working with Children and Families* by Forrester, Wilkins and Whittaker (2021).

Of course, none of this is to take away from or an attempt to reduce the feelings we experience in this role, such as impatience, sadness and frustration. I am not advocating for an approach that prohibits us from having feelings. Indeed, ensuring we have a space to share these feelings prevents them from unhelpfully being projected into our relationship with parents, thus undermining our intentions.

CHAPTER 6

Assessment: Making Meaning and Links

TOWARDS THE END OF A BUSY DAY, Terri, a mum of four children whom I have been working with for the past several months, rings me.

'Hi Rich, I was wondering if you know what the outcome of my assessment is going to be?'

'Terri, I've completed the assessment, and my manager has reviewed it, but it's currently with our solicitor for a final check. Tomorrow, I can come over and share the report's outcome with you.'

'I can't wait that long, please, it's not fair 'cus I will just be up all night with anxiety and stress. Please, Rich, can you just tell me what you have said?'

I hesitated, aware of the seriousness, but I couldn't uphold the normal process and replied, 'Terri, I really didn't want to do this over the phone, but I also don't want to keep you waiting any longer. I am really sorry but my recommendation is that the children can't come home.'

Silence followed the other end of the line. Eventually, she asked, 'Why not?'

'It's quite difficult to summarize a 30-page report, and I am happy to explain further when we meet tomorrow. It's related to your relationship with Max, and the impact that your mental health has on the children.'

'Okay, what time will you come round tomorrow?', Terri inquired.

'How about 2.30pm?' I suggested.

'Yeah, see you tomorrow, thank you, bye.'

'Bye, Terri' I said, before hanging up.

I leaned back, sank into my chair, looked up, closed my eyes and let out a sigh, as I thought to myself, 'Fucking hell, what a shit job... I wish she had been angry and told me to fuck off because that would have been more fitting to the situation, and truthfully, made me feel less bad.'

How ego-centric to make this about me.

I wish this wasn't my job as a social worker, but unfortunately, this is the reality of the child protection social work role. And part of that reality was that I had to have a conversation with Terri explaining that the assessment I had written recommended her children shouldn't return home. This meant the local authority care plan would be adoption for the younger two. The outcome of the report that I shared with Terri reveals, albeit at the extreme end of it, the important function of writing an assessment, and this is what I am going to look at in this chapter.

Why we write assessments

I didn't always comprehend this in the business of the job, but an assessment is an essential legal document. I had to make judgements about whether children were experiencing harm and consider whether they were eligible for support or required statutory involvement.

Therefore, an assessment is an evidential document identifying that the child has an identified need that meets the threshold for specialist intervention. It is a gateway to additional support and government resources that aren't available in the absence of assessed need (Section 17). Or it can be a document that evidences a level of harm that warrants statutory involvement in a child and family's life (Section 47), including recommendations for children to be removed. It should show that the social worker has been fair and proportionate in their approach, balancing the competing rights of children and adults, and incorporating their wishes and feelings to arrive at an informed decision.

To put it simply, assessment is about ethical, humane and rights-based social work.

There is also another reason for assessment. In Chapter 2, I recounted the feedback from my manager regarding how I had felt that Jacob and Ella would not be affected by domestic abuse because of their young age, and how that had resulted in me learning about brain development. What I wrote in that assessment reflected my knowledge about child development and domestic abuse, and how I applied that to Jacob and Ella influenced my judgement of risk, as well as the support we would provide the family. Writing it down so that others could review it allowed a critical process to occur, perhaps one of the most important processes: error detection.

If I had not written down what I had thought, or if that assessment had not been read by my manager who subsequently provided excellent feedback, then my knowledge and analysis of risk would have been left unchecked. However, writing the assessment and critically getting feedback allowed me to improve my thinking and my ability as a social worker. After 13 years of writing dozens, if not hundreds, of assessments, I still consider it the most effective way to improve my knowledge and skills as a social worker.

I often found it hard to think clearly about a family's situation because of the complexity of their presenting needs. I would collate information from various people, some more reliable than others. Sometimes I would be overwhelmed by the amount of information, and other times I had too little information. In addition to varying degrees of quality and quantity of information, the dynamics of my relationship I had with a family could influence my thoughts and feelings about them, and, in turn, affect my judgement about the level of risk. Some parents were kind, some were hostile; some were passive, some were passionate; some elicited sympathy, some provoked anger; some reminded me of my dad; and some parents I could see myself in.

In the midst of all of this, I was tasked with trying to make semi-coherent sense of the family in order to decide the extent of our involvement and, more importantly, what could be done to help the child. I learned, therefore, that an assessment is an opportunity to integrate these thoughts and feelings with the available evidence we have about the harm the children have experienced, as well as incorporate multiple perspectives, including those of professionals and family members. It is a crucial link between the problem and the solution. This involves holding up and analysing several strands of information simultaneously, identifying patterns or discrepancies, and forming an informed opinion.

Assessing parenting

I visited the home of Charlie (introduced in Chapter 2) and his younger brothers, Carter and Cain. Charlie, Carter and Cain lived with their mum, 22-year-old care leaver Leila, in a small, two-bedroom terraced house with their three cats, one hamster and two dogs. The smashed windowpane covered up with Sellotape and cardboard in the front door meant that I could anticipate the type of visit I would have based on the noise leaking out of the hole in the front door.

Leila opened the door, glanced at me, and walked back into the house without saying anything. I followed her through the hallway into the living area. A lifetime of social workers visiting her seemed to have resulted in a resigned acceptance or a passive indifference to our involvement. As I walked through the hall, I passed the kitchen, where I caught sight of a pile of dirty plates, pans and a dozen cups on the side, an overflowing bin bag, several flies swirling around it, and food and pieces of rubbish strewn across the floor. I sat in the living room, which was nicely furnished and decorated, but messy and cluttered.

Leila began reeling off problems she'd had with the neighbours, the complaints from school about Charlie's behaviour, and the stress she had had from her landlord, who had threatened her with eviction due to her rent arrears. To add to this, her car tyre had punctured while taking the children to school today.

As Leila rapidly listed off her current problems, Carter had made a game out of jumping off the arm of the sofa on one end and onto my lap. Initially, I caught him, fearing for his safety, but he took this as an act of reciprocation and repeated these leaps, which delighted him and terrified me. Meanwhile, Charlie played on his gaming device, occasionally providing a running commentary so detailed about a game I knew nothing about that he might as well have been speaking in another language. Cain floated around aimlessly, picking up toys and playing with them rudimentarily. At one point, he asked for crisps. Leila told him several times that he had had two packets already and he was about to have his tea soon. Sometimes she responded calmly and warmly, and other times she shouted at him, 'WILL YOU JUST STOP CAIN! I AM SICK OF SAYING NO, AND IF YOU ASK AGAIN, I WILL SEND YOU TO YOUR ROOM!'

Cain persisted for 35 minutes, and Leila eventually gave him some crisps. As all this unfolded, I sat there with my notepad to one side with the list of questions I had printed off to ask about her parenting, wondering how I would get a chance to ask these. Then Leila's friend, Carly, walked into the house. I introduced myself as the social worker, and she said 'Hi', apparently unphased by my presence.

'Alright Le?'

Leila replied, 'No, not really, my tyre burst this morning and I got no one to get the car or help me fix it.'

Carly said, 'Aw hun, that car is always causing you trouble.' Then she pivoted towards the kids, 'Right boys, Auntie Carly is taking you to the park. Who wants to come with me?'

The boys jumped up in synchrony and walked out happily with Carly.

Without the children, the house quickly felt eerily quiet. Leila said, 'I hate it when the children aren't here, it feels so empty', and I gained the impression that she felt uncomfortable in herself without the children creating noise and demanding her attention. Finally, though, I could ask Leila the questions I had prepared for the session.

When I asked about the children and their needs, she gave thoughtful, insightful answers about their need for warmth, routine, boundaries and protection. She told me about the different parenting courses she had attended, and proudly showed me several certificates. I asked about her on-off relationship with the children's father, Caleb, and she told me that she would never get back with him after he had recently tried to strangle her. She told me she needed to focus on the children because they deserved better.

She was thoroughly convincing. I wanted to believe her.

Leila had many strengths. First of all, she was very endearing and likeable. Second, she had endured more than most, and was a strong and inspiring person. Third, at times she showed Charlie, Carter and Cain exemplary emotional warmth, and could play with them beautifully. Fourth, she wanted her house to look nice, and although it was messy, she evidently tried hard to furnish and decorate it to a high standard. Finally, when I spoke with her, she had good ideas for how to raise the children, and aspired for them to have a childhood that most parents wished for – to be happy, healthy and achieve highly in school. When they grew up, she said she wanted them to get a good job, meet someone who treated them well and have a family. Nearly all the parents I have asked this question of have offered remarkably similar answers.

Despite these strengths, Charlie, Carter and Cain presented with significant emotional and behavioural issues. There were numerous concerns about the children being neglected or shouted at by Leila, and her relationship with Caleb was dangerously violent and characterized by them separating and then getting back together again.

Working with Leila confused me. Like most parents I worked with, her own ideas about parenting didn't always match up to the parenting she provided. In other words, she had good knowledge about her children and how to parent them, and yet, for various reasons, she was unable to provide this, at least consistently. This was linked to another problem I encountered frequently. Many parents had attended parenting courses. Some, like Leila, had participated in the same one a few times or attended several different types. So I couldn't understand why Leila still had trouble parenting Charlie, Carter and Cain. She had the knowledge and skills; at times, she could interact with her children heart-warmingly. There was no doubt she loved those boys.

After a while, I began to see that, paradoxically, parenting concerns weren't about parenting or knowledge about parenting. The parenting issues I observed were often (if not always) symptoms of an underlying problem. Charlie, Carter and Cain's problems were not because their mother didn't know what they needed or because she could not provide it. It was, I suspect, because Leila had been traumatized by her upbringing and had profound insecurities in her relationships with others. As a result, she seemed anxious, insecure and hypervigilant about being hurt, rendering her quick to react with defensive hostility.

To manage her intense and unresolved feelings, she smoked cannabis, which helped with some of her symptoms, but created other problems. She spent a lot of her money on drugs, and getting hold of and taking drugs took up her time and energy, which left her with less for her children. These underlying difficulties resulted in her care of Charlie, Carter and Cain being highly inconsistent and unpredictable, and the children all had to find ways of coping with this.

Therefore, in many instances, I found that it was underlying issues such as poor mental health, domestic abuse and substance misuse that caused some parents to function in a way that, despite their intentions regarding parenting, they struggled to consistently provide emotional warmth, routine, boundaries and safe care.

This realization had significant implications for how I approached assessments and helping families. I used to get caught up trying to solve all the symptoms and place inordinate expectations on myself. It meant that I would be trying to solve 10 to 15 issues simultaneously, which overwhelmed me and the families I was working with.

For example, I expected Leila to work with Citizens Advice, a one-to-one family support worker, attend a drug and alcohol service and a parenting course, work with an independent domestic violence advocate, attend the Freedom Programme, take the children to the dentist as well as meet with the health visitor and myself regularly. Some of these support services might have worked some of the time, but all of them would almost certainly not work, and so I set Leila and myself up to fail.

Assessment, therefore, is about finding the underlying issue, the main cause of concern. A helpful idea I came across from Crittenden is the 'critical cause of danger' and the 'critical cause of change' (2016, p.284), whereby we identify one or two underlying issues that, if resolved, would have a cascading effect on all the other issues. In my experience, these were domestic abuse, substance misuse, poor mental health and unresolved trauma. If I could collaborate with the parents about the underlying issue and support them with that, then the concerns for their parenting would be diminished, at least to a degree that meant the family didn't need statutory involvement.

What is an assessment?

Piecing it together, an assessment, I believe, has three components. First, it is how to assess whether a child is suffering significant harm, and to make an informed recommendation about whether to support the family under child in need or consider the child protection process. Or, in the case of parenting assessments, whether a child can safely remain living with their parents. Second, it is so a reasonable understanding of the problem can be developed and support identified that is tied to the cause of the concern. This requires searching for the underlying issue. And third, it is how the parent's capacity to change is assessed. I now explore these components in more detail.

Assessing the risk of harm

When I first started as a social worker, we used to have an Initial Assessment, which had to be completed within 10 days, and a Core Assessment, which had to be completed within 45 days. As I worked in the long-term team, I only completed Core Assessments.

The Core Assessment was developed by the Department of Health and organized around the assessment triangle – the child's needs, parenting capacity and family and environmental factors

– with different templates depending on the child's age. It was initially developed to address previous failures in adopting a holistic approach to the assessment of families, and was introduced shortly before I started work, in 2010.

Copyright © 'Triangle of Need' from the Department of Health's *Framework for the Assessment of Children in Need and Their Families* (2000). Used with permission.

In the template I used, there were several questions to ask a parent under each category within the three broad domains. These were 'Yes/No' questions with an option to add notes. For example, under child's health needs, questions included 'Child is normally well?', 'Child has a regular sleep pattern?', 'Child eats well?', 'Child frequently wets the bed?', etc. I recall there were many questions, and in writing this chapter, I looked up the Core Assessment and counted the number of questions. There were over 280!

And the electronic system I used, LCS (Liquidlogic Children's System), wouldn't allow you to complete the assessment if there was an unanswered question. As a student and newly qualified social worker I liked the Core Assessment. I had no clue how to conduct an assessment or what questions to ask, and so the Core Assessment solved that problem for me.

It also allowed me to ask questions I would otherwise feel uncomfortable asking, such as 'Child is hit?' By telling a parent that I would be asking a series of questions from this form, it depersonalized the process and made me feel more at ease asking difficult questions. This was where I learned about the value of asking questions, which I think is the most valuable tool in the social worker's toolbox.

Finally, it gave me a series of questions I could ask other professionals about the child – for example, the education section questions include 'Child's educational progress is satisfactory?', 'Child is happy to go to school?', 'Child attends school regularly?', 'Child arrives on time?', and 'Child has friend at school?' These are questions that I still use today. They are essential because they provide factual evidence about the child's educational outcomes.

One key learning early on was separating fact from opinion, and even clarifying facts. For example, a teacher might say, 'Joe is constantly getting into fights with his peers', which could be accepted, or it might then be helpful to ask, 'How often is Joe getting into fights?', 'On average, is it a few times a week, once per week, once per month?', 'Is it with the same peers?', 'What type of fights are they?', 'Do you know what the fights are about?', 'Is there anything you could do to support Joe in getting into fewer fights?'

Another example might be that Laura 'is doing fine at school', and when you ask about her attendance and educational attainment, you learn that her attendance is 92 per cent, that she is painfully shy, has few friends, and is working below average in Maths, Science and English. Or you learn her attendance is 98 per cent, she is working at age-related expectations for Maths and above for Science and English, and she has a lovely, positive group of friends.

Separating fact from opinion was also a skill I learned to apply in my assessment writing. For example, I would avoid using phrases like 'Poor home conditions', 'Emotional and behavioural problems', 'Drinks a lot' – not because they weren't true, but because they all contain subjective language, which is then open to interpretation. What 'poor', 'problems' and 'a lot' mean will depend on the person reading it. Therefore, where possible, I would use descriptive language. For example, 'Joe's bedroom had a bed, with no bed sheet or quilt cover. There was little floor space, as it was mostly covered by empty crisp packets, dirty clothes and broken toys. He had no curtains, and had drawn all over the walls.'

Learning from Munro

However, while the Core Assessment provided me some reassurance as a newly qualified social worker, and supplied me with lots of useful questions, I eventually found that it had some limitations. For example, I didn't always know what to do with all the information unless the concerns were blatantly obvious. In her book *Effective Child Protection* (2008), Eileen Munro's writing on this proved instructive.

First, she detailed four key questions to ask in any assessment: (1) What is or has happened? (2) What might happen? (3) How likely are these outcomes? (4) How undesirable are they? Answering these four questions from the child's perspective formed the basis for my analysis. Munro also posited that an overall judgement of risk was a combination of likelihood and desirability. For example, one case might have a high probability of the children being subject to harm, yet with mild to moderately undesirable outcomes (such as some cases of neglect). In contrast, another case might be considered to have a low probability of abuse or harm occurring, yet highly undesirable outcomes (such as some cases of non-accidental injury).

Second, Munro argues that there are two ways of collating information. First is our intuition, which can include our first impression of someone, how they make us feel, and our gut instincts. Most social workers will have had the experience of entering a home, and even though there is nothing obvious to be worried about, they will have a feeling that 'something isn't quite right'. That is our gut instinct, which works quickly and without much thinking – so quickly, in fact, that we have the feeling before we have thought about the feeling. The second way is formal and analytical, which involves using questionnaires, not unlike the Core Assessment, and other more formal ways to collect information.

These two ways of collecting and understanding information are sometimes pitched against each other, framed as a question: is social work an art or a science? Munro persuasively argues that both are valid and we should ideally use both. But importantly, we should recognize the strengths and limitations of using both, so we can make the most out of each approach. Our intuition, Munro points out, while fast and helpful at times, is subject to flaws and can mislead us regarding the level of risk a child might be at. On the other hand, formal analytical methods can help mitigate some of those biases and improve our objectivity, although they can be slow and time-consuming.

Understanding the biases that influenced my judgement profoundly impacted how capable I thought I was in making reliable, rational judgements. This confidence speaks to the first bias, overconfidence, which is the tendency to believe that our abilities are better than they are. One of the most important pieces of advice I received from one of my managers was 'confidence over competence is dangerous', and nowhere is that truer than in child protection social work.

Relatedly, there is confirmation bias, a strong tendency to find or filter only the information that supports our pre-existing view or a conclusion we have made. In other words, once we have formed a view, we find it extremely difficult to accept information contrary to this view. The strength of this bias is such that Munro argues that 'The single most important factor in minimizing errors [in child protection] is to admit you may be wrong' (2008, p.125). Thank goodness! I have often changed my assessment of the level of risk a child is experiencing during supervision – nothing objective has changed, but my interpretation of the available information has altered through exploration of these issues with my manager. Availability bias is the tendency to give disproportionate value to sensory input or information presented vividly compared with plain, dryly presented information.

Next is the *halo effect*, which is the tendency to judge a person's entire character based on one aspect of their appearance or presentation. For example, when I first met Leila and observed her interact warmly with her children, I found it hard to acknowledge or even believe the reports I had read about her shouting or being abusive towards her children.

A similar, if not identical, idea to the halo effect was outlined in an old social work book by Robert Dingwall and his colleagues called *The Protection of Children* (1995). In observing social workers in the 1980s they found that if parents had extremely 'limited capacities' (e.g., were severely neglectful) and caused evidential harm to their children, this could be overlooked if they showed love ('natural love') (1995, p.94). Reflecting on my practice with Leila and other parents similarly capable of demonstrating high levels of emotional warmth, I noticed that I would unintentionally overlook the harm their parenting had on their children.

The final bias, and in my opinion the most important, is called What You See Is All There Is, or WYSIATI , described in Daniel Kahneman's book, *Thinking Fast and Slow* (2011). This is a bias in which we make judgements of a situation based on the coherence of an explanation we have conjured up, and not based on the quality or quantity of the information. We build a story from the available information, even if it's poor quality, and if it's a good story, we believe it. However, we don't consider the information we don't know or that might be missing.

When a parent told me that she was going to leave her domestically abusive partner, I believed her: what you see is all there is. When a parent was emotionally warm with their child, I found it hard to imagine they could be suffering significant harm: what you see is all there is. When I visited the clean, tidy and well-furnished home of a parent chronically addicted to heroin, I found it hard to imagine her children being neglected: what you see is all there is.

The chronology (do not skip!)

What surprised me when I learned about these biases was that very little can be done to avoid them. They are habitual and automatic; nobody is immune from them. However, there are tools that we can use in assessing children and families to counteract some of the effects of these biases. And the tool that has been the most helpful over the years has been the chronology. When I first qualified, however, the chronology was, as far as I could tell, a needless bureaucratic exercise that deprived me of time for the 'real' work with children and families. And yet, I was asked to do one on every single case!

However, while begrudgingly trawling through the multiple children's case files, I learned some valuable lessons. I discovered five reasons for undertaking a chronology.

1. To understand children's social care involvement with the family or child so far

Some families I worked with had very little social work involvement previously, and others had extensive involvement, and this impacted on our relationship. To caricature the differences, parents with little involvement tended to be anxious and fearful, whereas parents with a lot of involvement tended to be indifferent (perhaps unimpressed with our offer of 'help'), or skilled at saying what needed to be said to avoid any additional scrutiny.

When I wrote a chronology and summarized every referral, assessment, strategy meeting, legal meeting, and, if relevant, care proceedings, I could see parents' responses to different social workers across time.

'He's taken it too far this time, Rich, and for the children, I am not willing to put up with him anymore; he can hit me, but hitting them is the last straw. If he wants to see the children, I won't stop him seeing the children, never have, never will. I didn't see my dad growing up and I know what it's like, but he will need to go to a contact centre.'

Ruby told me this while Isabelle cuddled into her, quietly wiping her tears from her face. There was no doubt in my mind that she meant it this time. I was sympathetic for her courage and bravery, liaised with several professionals, arranged for the police to improve the security of her home, explored refuge options, and made a referral for domestic abuse support.

When I reviewed the chronology, however, I learned that this was how Ruby had responded for the last several incidents. Each time the social worker took similar steps to what I had done before closing the case, assuming that the risk in the family home had reduced. That didn't negate the appropriateness of the support I provided Ruby, because it can often take several attempts before someone ends an abusive relationship – it's probably sensible to treat every attempt as the attempt that will succeed. But it changed my assessment of the probability of future harm and reorientated the support to think about what help could be provided if Ruby reunited with her partner.

2. To understand patterns of behaviour, such as domestic abuse, substance misuse, neglect etc.

John, in his 20s, was tall and broad-shouldered. I was warmly welcomed into his home, and he was chatty, funny and at times charming. I didn't feel this was a deliberate putting-on-a-show, but rather an aspect of his personality.

'I know I have messed up, and I am not saying that what I did in that relationship with Anna was good, but I was in a bad way, taking shit loads of cocaine with her and, and, the relationship was just toxic, do you know what I mean, Rich...oh, shit, hang on, I am so sorry, Rich I didn't even offer you a drink did I, do you want a cup of tea or a coffee or anything?'

'I am okay, thank you.'

'That's alright mate, if you change your mind just let me know, so anyway, I am actually a big softie, I even bought Ava-Louise one of those massive teddy bears at the fair the other day [chuckle]. I just can't help myself, you should of seen the look on her face, though, Rich, absolutely priceless, and that's what I am about now. I know I have done some naughty things, we all have, haven't we? I bet you have, haven't you, Rich?', he asked rhetorically.

'But that was back then, I was a completely different person then, unrecognizable. I bumped into me old pal Charlie the other day and he was like "Bloody hell Johnny, you look so different" and I said, "I know mate, I am getting my life back on track", and literally everyone I bump into says the same thing. That was the thing with me and Anna, absolutely brought the worst out of each. We were like dynamite. We loved each other, don't get me wrong, she was the light of my life. I never loved someone as much as I loved that girl and then she completely destroyed me. Is this making sense? Sorry, I am just desperate to be with Ava-Louise. I would be absolutely crushed if I couldn't see her. She's my bright star [starts crying] and I fucking love that girl. Sorry to swear, but I just don't what I would do without her. Do you think I got chance then, Rich? What do you reckon because the last social worker just read about me on paper and then made her mind up. You're not like though are you, Rich, are you? I can tell you're decent.'

When John spoke, he maintained clear and direct eye contact, and with an apparent frankness. He asked questions that sought agreement, and with such passion and conviction, it was difficult to resist the temptation to agree with everything he said. I also felt apprehensive about not agreeing, sensing, subconsciously, that disagreeing would be unwise. His evocative and powerful statements about his love for Ava-Louise were genuine and heartfelt, but also slightly over the top. His compliments were effective, even though I realized they were given as a way to try and get me on his side, and that he was pitching me against the previous social worker. Being a dad myself, I empathized with his wish to be in his daughter's life, and I was sensitive to some of the negative stereotypes against men and their role as parents. I left the visit inspired to advocate for John's proactive involvement with Ava-Louise.

In writing the chronology for John, however, a very different picture emerged. His account of the 'toxic relationship' with Anna and past 'naughty things' that he wanted me to agree we all had done amounted to several incidents of dangerous – often drug-induced – violence against Anna, including strangling her unconscious, knocking her teeth out and hospitalizing her with a head injury after he had thrown a vase at her while she was pregnant.

I also discovered that domestic abuse featured in all his previous relationships. And even before that, there were multiple incidents of violence against his mother when he was a teenager. Additionally, he had been involved in several altercations with neighbours, work colleagues and strangers during nights out. For the offences he was charged for, he had breached several orders, and was often recalled to court or prison.

John had an extensive history of substance misuse, and although he claimed abstinence, the hair strand drug test revealed ongoing alcohol and cocaine use. When I asked John, he said, 'I only have a little bit [of cocaine] on a Friday. Literally everyone does. I even know social workers, lawyers and police that do. I only do when I don't have Ava-Louise, and to be honest, I only probably do because I don't have her. I am so upset about not seeing her all the time that it just takes my mind off it.'

Munro points out that 'the best predictor of future behaviour is past behaviour' (Munro 2008, p.77). When I started, I felt uneasy about using past behaviour to judge future behaviour because it seemed unethical. And I wanted to hold on to the belief that people can change; indeed, I felt that much of the good fortune I have experienced is because I was given a chance and not unduly judged by my past.[1]

This optimism for parents' capacity to change could be considered a bias, what I call a 'positive outlook on change bias' (not as catchy as the scientifically validated biases). I think the 'positive outlook on change bias' is a useful interpersonal tool because I think it is important, if not morally necessary, that we convey to parents that we believe they can change, even when the odds are stacked against them. But in terms of assessing risk of harm, it is perhaps less helpful.

---

[1] In the third edition of *Effective Child Protection*, Munro added to this quote and the newer, fully extended version is, 'the best predictor of future behaviour is past behaviour (though people can and do also change)', to prevent it being used as an absolute rule (2019, p.147).

Another difficulty I encountered was that parents would often convincingly describe how their situation was different and how they had changed, but their reasons for this might vary. Sometimes, this was because they had made the changes. Sometimes, like in Ruby's case, she genuinely meant that she had changed at that moment. But after a short while – perhaps when she felt lonely or wanted help with the children – she reconciled the relationship. Sometimes, parents want to make the changes but haven't done so. And sometimes, like in John's case, they don't believe their past behaviour was harmful and don't understand or see the need to change, or only say they do because they think it is what social workers want to hear.

Therefore, evaluating the probability of harm requires exploring factors other than the quality of our relationship with a parent and their expressed commitment towards change, which returns us to Munro's argument.

In reviewing past behaviour, I think there are three key variables to consider, most of which can be drawn out from the chronology:

- *Duration.* This provides information on how long the pattern of behaviour has been in place (the longer the pattern has been in place, the less likelihood of spontaneous change). John had been using intimidation, aggression and violence as a way of managing his feelings and relationships with others since he was a teenager. Therefore it was unlikely that he would change. It wasn't impossible, but it was unlikely.
- *Severity of the pattern.* This provides information on how entrenched and problematic the behaviour is and the support that will be required. John had demonstrated that he could be violent and cause serious injury to the people he loved, irrespective of who was there, such as his children. This speaks to the severity of his problem, compared to, for example, someone who could occasionally lose their temper but never resort to physical violence. To give another example, two parents could suffer from depression, and one of them feel low and unmotivated one or two days a week, whereas

ASSESSMENT: MAKING MEANING AND LINKS   117

another parent could be debilitated, unable to get out of bed and leave the home.

- *Frequency.* This provides information on the severity of the problem, the impact on functioning and whether an issue is improving or deteriorating. John was frequently involved in incidents with others, resulting in him reacting aggressively and violently. This meant that Ava-Louise would be repeatedly exposed to scary and frightening incidents. There was also no evidence that the frequency of incidents in the past several months had reduced.

Of course, the caveat to using the past to judge future behaviour is that people can change at any time. A parent who has misused heroin for 20 years can decide to end that addiction in an instant. Reviewing and analysing a parent's history doesn't preclude the possibility of change, but it does provide important clues, probably the most valuable clues we have, about whether change is likely or not. Patterns that manifest in different contexts or across time are predicted to be more resistant to change. Conversely, patterns that are context-specific are more likely to change, especially if the context that facilitated the pattern changes.

In thinking about change, then, the stronger the evidence that the behaviour is chronic, entrenched and frequently interfering with their parenting, the more substantial the evidence we need to see that change has occurred. For John, who had managed his emotions and relationships with aggression and violence for two decades in multiple contexts (family relationships, work, neighbours), and who had been impervious to legal consequences, the probability of change was very low despite his impassioned and persuasive pleas during my visit to him. To be convinced otherwise would require a significant period of time where concern for his violent tendencies wasn't an issue, and ideally (although not always necessary) evidence that he had engaged in the appropriate support that would bring about change.

3. To understand the support that has been provided and the impact that it has had

When I was working with Jackie and her four children (the twins, Billy and Ben, and Jolene and Jade – described back in Chapter 4), we had developed a plan based on the presenting issues, such as parenting courses, support for domestic abuse and Jackie's mental health. In reviewing the chronology, I discovered that Jackie had already attended three parenting courses. Indeed, I had also referred her on to another parenting course several weeks earlier. Each time a new social worker was allocated, like me, they would look at the presenting issues without reviewing the history, and make referrals to the relevant support agencies. There would be mild improvements; the social worker would end involvement, only for further concerns to re-emerge. A new social worker would be allocated, and the same process would be initiated. I had fallen into the same trap and began to see a similar pattern in many other cases when undertaking a chronology.

I was duplicating the work that had already been done by previous social workers, which was a massive waste of time and a completely ineffective use of support services. It also set Jackie up to fail, because if the course hadn't worked the first three times, it was unlikely the fourth time would make a difference. As the famous quote – often misattributed to Albert Einstein – goes, 'Insanity is doing the same thing over and over again but expecting different results'.

Therefore, reviewing the support provided allowed me to understand what support had already been provided, and whether it had had the intended outcomes. If it hadn't, the question was whether this was because of poor engagement, and had this been a pattern throughout previous involvement? Or did the parent engage in the support, and it hadn't had the intended outcome? If the latter, this could indicate that we had offered the wrong support. Perhaps we had misunderstood the difficulties in the family.

ASSESSMENT: MAKING MEANING AND LINKS 119

4. To understand the child's experiences and the impact of harm on them

Joseph was a large 13-year-old boy with scruffy, uncut, brown hair, often seen in a large, oversized hoody, shorts (no matter the season) and expensive trainers. He was sweet, polite and easy to get along with. Joseph was on the precipice of being permanently excluded from school for low-level but persistently disruptive behaviour. His poor behaviour wasn't because he was a 'bad' kid, but as a way of him dealing with insecurity and anxiety around fitting in. Joseph had few friends and was lonely. At home, his parents, Ella and Paul, felt that he was despondent. He would spend most nights awake into the early hours of the morning, numbing himself with his two vices, gaming and food. He had also suffered from incontinence issues, which compounded his poor self-esteem and had been a past source of bullying.

Ella and Paul presented as conscientious, concerned parents. They were especially worried after finding out that he had been watching violent pornography, and had confiscated his phone. They often speculated over a diagnosis, and while they were mostly sympathetic, Paul could be dismissive about Joseph's feelings, asking professionals to 'fix him' and 'find out what is wrong with him'. Ella and Paul had a younger child who was flourishing, reinforcing the idea that in their mind, the problem was in Joseph, that there was something wrong with him.

In writing the chronology, I learned that Ella was 17 when she had given birth to Joseph, and her relationship with Paul was incredibly volatile. Several incidents had resulted in police attendance, and their relationship had ended when Joseph was two years old, after Paul was imprisoned for several drugs-related offences. Paul spent the next two years in and out prison, getting clean while he was inside, and quickly picking up his habit once he was released. During this period Paul would often arrange to see Joseph, only to cancel at the last minute. The health visitor supported Ella at this time, who suffered from depression and anxiety. She told the health visitor that with everything going on she was struggling to bond with Joseph. Paul eventually achieved sobriety, which he maintained after being released from prison when Joseph was four. Ella and Paul reconciled, and together established a happy, stable life for themselves.

The chronology, therefore, provided a development context for some of Joseph's behaviours, which had previously not made sense.

I found that a chronology can be one of the most effective ways to understand the child's lived experience across their life span, and in particular, it allows us to examine the child's reaction and response to incidents of harm (e.g., where the child was during a domestic abuse incident, what they saw, heard and how they talked about it afterwards).

It can also support understanding of the trajectory of the child's development. If, for example, a child's emotional and behavioural presentation worsens year by year, then we can make some reasonable predictions about their future outcomes if change does not occur.

5. To identify strengths in the family and exceptions

The final lesson I took from writing chronologies was that I found gaps where there were no referrals or children's social care involvement. Sometimes, we don't become involved until a child is much older. Or we are involved with a family and then we are not involved again for a few years before we are again. Finding these gaps provides opportunities to explore and develop an understanding of past examples and times when the parents or the wider family system have been able to manage more successfully.

With this understanding, we can use the family's pre-existing coping strategies and strengths to improve children's safety. Improving outcomes in child protection for children involves minimizing risks *and/or* improving safety. Indeed, as we will explore in the next chapter, we can sometimes create enough safety for children by focusing solely on enhancing strengths without changing the risk factors.

Undertaking the chronology changed from being one of the many meaningless and time-wasting exercises in the highly procedural machinery of the child protection system to being *the* most powerful, evidentially robust and effective way to understand a child's experiences and assess the risk of harm. It is undoubtedly time-consuming, but I think it saves disproportionately more time in the long run. It saves time lost by offering the same support and attempting the same approaches to help the family. And time lost by closing a case only for it to reopen a few weeks later (resulting in a revolving door situation) when it could have been predicted and avoided. Writing assessments was much easier with access to all the key information on one document, rather than spread across the child's electronic file.

Identifying underlying issues

So far, I have described the process of assessing whether a child is at risk of harm. This involves recognizing the role of cognitive biases, the use of questions and the importance of the chronology, particularly the five elements involved in chronology. I now look at assessing underlying patterns because, as I mentioned at the beginning of this chapter, this can help us get to the root cause of a parent's difficulties. Undertaking a chronology is one way; talking to parents about their childhood and life experiences is another.

I've always believed that people are fundamentally good and want to live a healthy, happy life. Therefore, when people behave in ways that are harmful to themselves or others, I assume something must have happened to derail them. For example, when I first qualified, I was intrigued by parents who thought that the best way to maintain a relationship with a loved one was through coercion, control and violence. I wondered how they had concluded that this was how to sustain a relationship when it clearly made the person they loved deeply afraid, unfulfilled and sometimes injured. If it was their attempt to maintain a relationship, it seemed counterproductive because it was guaranteed to drive the other person away. I also assumed that being the type of person who hurts another, emotionally or physically, couldn't be good for their self-esteem and well-being.

I have found two benefits to exploring a parent's upbringing. First, once I understood their background and realized that behaviour that was destructive or harmful, when understood in the context of their lived experiences, made more sense – was rational even – this was a basis for compassion, which helped my relationship with them. Second, it provided insight into the underlying nature of their difficulties, which would provide clues for the type of support needed.

After examining a parent's childhood, the second key area was exploring their adult relationships (looking for links between childhood and adulthood). Over the years, I have noticed two different patterns. First is like John, where the parent repeatedly perpetrates violence and control, but denies, minimizes and provides persuasive extenuating reasons or circumstances to justify the violence. These individuals struggle to accept responsibility and apportion blame to others, and lack awareness of their behaviour's impact on others. Failing to see how their behaviour impacts others and justifying violence as necessary due to perceived unavoidable circumstances makes it difficult for them to change their behaviour.

John's Adult Attachment Interview would likely reveal an experience of highly unpredictable parenting, danger and rejection. In this context, he had learned to mistrust others and expect deception and rejection. To cope with this, he might have developed a self-protective strategy that involved being anxious, needy, fearful and pre-emptive of rejection or danger.

Second is like Jackie (from Chapter 4), where the parent is repeatedly victimized by abusive partners. They find themselves in unhealthy and abusive partnerships, and sustain these relationships even when self-evidently abusive and harmful. This usually reflects a profound sense of low self-worth and poor self-esteem, where they don't believe they deserve to be treated positively, and so unconsciously select partners who reinforce those underlying beliefs about themselves. Sometimes they take responsibility for the abuse, in part internalizing the blame for the abuse, and this can lead them to paint the misleading picture that it is reciprocal.[2]

---

2   Of course, no one is responsible for the abuse or violence other than the perpetrator; responsibility lies entirely with them. Ideally, we would live in a world where there weren't individuals who acted in abusive and violent ways so that there wouldn't be domestic abuse, whether someone had poor self-esteem or not. This perspective also isn't instead of systemic issues that contribute to violence and oppression, but rather an addition.

ASSESSMENT: MAKING MEANING AND LINKS 123

Remember that when I did Jackie's Adult Attachment Interview she had learned to dismiss her feelings and needs and expect mistreatment, and had never experienced love within a safe relationship? Not uncommonly, these two patterns attract each other.

I will use John and Jackie as an imaginary couple for a moment. When I first qualified, I used to think that if only Jackie left John all the risk would be removed, and we wouldn't need to be involved. John, the perpetrator of violence, would leave the family home, and all would be well. Sometimes I actively encouraged this plan. If the risk escalated, we would ask them to sign a written agreement preventing contact between John and Jackie, or only permit it when the children were in school. More often than not, these agreements were breached (in other words, they were ineffective), which I would get frustrated about. Honestly, I would feel disappointed with parents like Jackie for not helping us help them.

These protective measures also had unintended consequences. I found that my attempts to safeguard the child and police the relationship would drive it underground. The parents didn't want to separate but seemingly went along with what I asked of them. In some cases, this increased the risk as both parents would be less inclined to seek support for fear of reprisals. So, ongoing domestic abuse would occur, albeit we wouldn't know about it (until we did!). Another unintended consequence was that even if Jackie and John stuck to the agreement, or we managed to push John out of the family system, this could sometimes have serious effects on the children who missed their father.

Although they were protected from the effects of domestic abuse, they were harmed and emotionally affected by the loss of their dad. In some instances, it wasn't clear what was worse – the domestic abuse or the loss of their dad and their family structure. The remaining parent (often the mother) would be left grieving for the loss of her relationship, adapting to being a single parent, and trying to support her children's distress for the loss of their father and the current instability.

In addition, I saw some parents like Jackie end the relationship with a partner under pressure from social care, but in the absence of being supported with her self-esteem and self-worth, she would end up in another relationship with someone equally abusive. Similarly, parents like John, although no longer harming the children I was responsible for, were now working with my colleague after he met another mother with two children and, after two weeks of being with her, had moved into the family home.

Underpinning this approach was the way I viewed parents. I overlooked them as individuals with their own needs and desires, and instead looked at them solely as parents who could ensure their children's safety or not. This hindered my relationship and ability to support them.

When I was 17 years old, I was walking with one of my friends, Lizzie, to meet some of our friends. Lizzie's mother had died several years earlier, and she hadn't known her father. Lizzie lived with her aunt and uncle, who owned a pub down south, but during the holidays she would stay with her mum's best friend, who lived a few doors down from me. At 16, she was in a relationship with someone twice her age, who looked three times her age, and, according to Lizzie, was an alcoholic. As we were walking to meet our friends, I asked her, 'Why are you with him when he is so much older than you?' I was naïve and confused about why she would want to be with him. She replied quickly and matter-of-factly, 'No one else will have me.' I've reflected on that brief conversation a lot since, and although I can't be sure, I wondered, from her vantage point and in light of her experiences, whether she thought this older male was her only opportunity for comfort, physical and sexual affection.

Lizzie didn't feel she had the option between a young, healthy, well-adjusted male her age or a much older, alcoholic male. It was the choice between nothing and something. I have found this true for many of the parents I have worked with – the fear of loneliness or abandonment is so intense and unbearable that they compromise their safety, and sometimes their children's safety, in pursuit of love and affection.

When I first qualified, I rarely, if ever, considered a parent's desire for sex, comfort and companionship when dealing with domestic abuse. If the relationship was harmful for the children, the solution was straightforward: end the relationship. In *Re-imagining Child Protection* by Professor Brid Featherstone, Professor Sue White and Professor Kate Morris, they point out that:

> Social Workers [like me!] focus primarily on behavioural changes to parenting practices, failing to explore what holds destructive relationships in place. For example, what role is played by sex and desire? In the relentless focus on risk and danger, have we lost the capacity as social workers to talk about desire, it's seductions and its perils? (2014, p.124)

This evolved (and evolving) understanding adjusted my practice because I was more mindful of the consequences of pursuing separation, willing to tolerate risk within the parents' relationship, and attempted to work with both parents on their respective issues. Working with them on their problems was greatly aided when I understood their background and acknowledged their survivorship and ability to adapt to past adverse events.

It also influenced the assessment of capacity to change, which I will explore next.

Assessing change

When I first qualified, I worked in an old, run-down town hall with thin, stained carpets that had single-pane windows that allowed little light, but plenty of chill, to seep in. In our office, which housed approximately 15 desks, we had a fridge, a microwave and a kettle. Not too infrequently, we had the radio playing in the background. It was an office, an ancient office, but one with all the home comforts. However, this was all to change. Responding to health and safety regulations, the council decided that individual kettles were no longer allowed in each office. Instead, there would be a small kitchenette area at the end of the corridor with access to an urn that all the individual offices could share. Chaos ensued after this.

The unexpected loss of our cherished kettle stirred outrage among us. No longer could we enjoy the simple pleasure of making a cup of tea within the comfort of our own office. Alliances formed, whispers of potential resignations circulated, a new item graced the team meeting agenda, and formal letters of disgruntlement found their way to senior managers. Nothing happened, of course. Within a few weeks, we had all forgotten and adjusted to our new set-up. The lesson here is that change is hard, even for social workers. And we all especially dislike change imposed on us, rather than when we are part of the decision-making and it is undertaken within our time frames.

Assessing the capacity to change is especially hard in child protection. Some parents fear (quite understandably) that failing to change or appear as though they are changing could result in escalating social work involvement. Therefore, some parents might say they have changed to get social workers out of their lives, or they might engage in support services not because they believe they need to or want to change, but because they worry about the consequences of not engaging.

Taking into consideration this challenge, I have found there are three key elements to assessing capacity to change. The first is to identify the key issues that need changing, usually substance misuse, neglect and domestic abuse. The second is to assess the pattern of behaviour that needs changing. The third is to provide access to support that will aid change.

A key distinction, however, is that engagement with support services isn't evidence of change. A parent can engage in every course under the sun and still not change. The fact that a parent is engaging in support services is a positive indicator, but it doesn't equate to behavioural change or improved safety for their child. That might be an outcome, but it is far from guaranteed. Equally, a parent might not engage in any of the support and still make the necessary changes. The fundamental aspect that requires attention and assessment is behavioural change – how has the child's lived experience changed?

Conclusion

Assessment is the defining feature of child protection social work. It demands our very best interpersonal skills, emotional resilience and intellect. The quality of the assessment is contingent, in part, on our ability to cultivate a collaborative relationship with parents. We need to generate trust and help them appreciate the worth of opening their lives to us. This carries many risks for parents. Yet, when a mutually satisfactory partnership can be established, we can better understand their difficulties, and hopefully be better positioned to help them and their children.

CHAPTER 7

Helping Children and Families

I ENTERED PETER AND ALISON'S TWO-BEDROOM HOME. Peter and Alison had two children, Alex and Hermione. It was one of the first cases I had been allocated as a newly qualified social worker. Peter and Alison's welcoming response reassured me as I sat nervously on the sofa, wearing my new, smart, black shoes, black trousers, and shirt. I had even purchased an informal briefcase as I thought a backpack would signify a lack of seriousness (or a schoolboy-ish appearance).

Having grown up poor and feeling ashamed for not having decent, well-fitted clothes and trainers, or being able to afford a regular haircut, I compensated for this as soon as I could afford to. I was also aware that I was a young, immature-looking 22-year-old, so I wanted to offset this with more formal attire to avoid not being taken seriously.

Peter began explaining how they had disagreed over money lately and how their arguments had gotten out of hand, resulting in him going to the pub, getting drunk, and coming home to argue with Alison. The neighbour called the police, and after hurling abuse at the police officers, he was arrested. Alison sighed and said she had had enough of Peter, who she felt was too controlling, spending all the money on cannabis, and expecting her to do all the housework. Peter swung side to side on his office chair in front of his desktop, which he spent hours in front of, gaming until the early hours of

129

the morning. He then explained that several years before he had been involved in an accident at work – he had broken both his legs and fractured his back. He hadn't been able to work since and had since sunk into depression, and found cannabis and gaming his only distractions.

As I sat there listening attentively, I thought, 'I've no idea how I am going to help Peter and Alison. They are old enough to be my parents, and who am I to suggest what they should or shouldn't do?'

They seemed utterly oblivious to my underlying anxiety and self-talk about the unfolding situation. They seemed to accept the façade of a competent professional rather than what I felt – a barely eligible adult who had just left university and started in my new role. I was busy figuring out how my experiences had affected me, what constituted a healthy relationship, and how to manage my addictive tendencies, and yet here they were, taking me seriously.

I left their home feeling touched and privileged that they were willing to share private details of their intimate life and relationship with one another with me. But I had no idea how to support and help them.

When I first qualified, I didn't understand how to help parents and children. Reflecting on this, this isn't surprising given the complexity of what we are asked to do (although at the time I felt the pressure to have all the answers). In this chapter, I will explore the lessons I gained in helping children and families, how that evolved after I learned Signs of Safety, and the lessons I have acquired since then.

Real, effective help

First, I learned that the elements of the job where I felt like I was 'helping' the most were few and far between, and were, in fact, not that helpful overall.

Ella, a 23-year-old mum of three children, had moved into the area I worked in after fleeing domestic abuse. She was isolated from her family, and while a committed and loving parent to her three boys, she lived a chaotic life where every day was a rollercoaster of emotions depending on what was happening in her life.

Some days she received an eviction notice and secured funding for her middle child to go to nursery. The next day, she would get into a dispute with a neighbour about the noise the children were making and then receive a back payment for overdue benefits, allowing her to purchase expensive Christmas presents for the children. One day, she had to stay in hospital for emergency dental treatment after the infected tooth she had masked for several weeks with illicit codeine became severely infected.

Every time I visited Ella, there was something to do. I would drive her to the chemist to pick up a prescription, pick up her son from nursery, go to the housing office with her, or play with her children while she was on the phone to Citizens Advice. While undertaking these activities, I felt good. I felt like I was making a positive difference. My relationship with Ella was great, and she always appreciated the support.

However, spending 2–3 hours taking Ella to the chemist or collecting her son from nursery, while enjoyable and personally rewarding, wasn't a sustainable way to manage my time – especially in light of all the other families I was working with. I realized that I could ask a family support worker to spend time helping Ella establish a routine, learn ways to manage money and finances, and occasionally take her to appointments. Sure, it was less rewarding personally, but it was where I could leverage my role to make a bigger difference for Ella and her children, and ultimately, that was my job.

Case management

I discovered that my role as a social worker wasn't necessarily to be a therapist or a family support worker. Instead, my role was to use my knowledge, skills and relationship to undertake assessments, identify relevant support services and refer parents to them, develop and review plans, and humanely and transparently let parents know about the relevant processes in respect of our involvement.

Indeed, one unacknowledged intervention is simply the implementation of a child protection plan, the pre-proceedings process or care proceedings. The shocking and stark realization that parents might lose their children can be a motivator for change, jolting some out of a stupor into taking action to turn their lives around. In these instances, I can take minimal credit for facilitating this change. From the parents' perspective, I am not a source of motivation or support, but rather an antagonist who has spurred them into action.

Unfortunately, this unromantic and uninspiring framing of our work turns a lot of social workers off the job as they realize, once they enter the profession, that they don't have time to do the work they imagined. But child protection social work as a form of rights-based case coordination – in contrast to unattainable, idealized notions of relationship-based practice – in my opinion should be celebrated as a noble, worthwhile and fundamentally important role that improves the lives of children and families. I believe this to be true, not based on practice experience, but because of my encounter with a social worker as a child.

When I was 11, a social worker came to our house. I was escorted into the living room, where we sat opposite a middle-aged woman with white, curly hair, leaning forward with her arms crossed over a notepad covering her knees. She asked several questions about my life, and then I was allowed to leave after a short while. At the time, I had no idea why she had visited or what the purpose was. I never saw her again.

Looking back, however, I suspect the social worker undertook an initial assessment that came about due to my dad being in rehab for his drug and alcohol use and my mum suffering from depression and chronic fatigue syndrome. A few weeks later, I began attending an organization called Young Carers. Through Young Carers I attended weekly groups where we did fun activities and group work (and I filled out many wishes and feelings sheets I would subsequently use with children in my role as a social worker). I also went on activity days during half-terms, and a few times I went on a residential trip in the summer holidays.

As I got older, I was provided with one-to-one counselling. At 16 years old, when I was too old to continue attending Young Carers, I was offered a role as a volunteer, which essentially allowed me to continue accessing this support while also pretending that I was helping and giving back. This voluntary position was a vital learning experience that helped me when I applied to college to undertake my BTEC National Diploma in Health and Social Care.

I learned as an adult that I had attended Young Carers because the social worker who had visited all those years before had made a referral for me to attend. I hope this doesn't sound too dramatic, but that social worker changed my life. She didn't try to intervene herself, or even change my parents. Rather, she identified a need and made a referral to a service that could provide long-term, quite intensive, and ultimately therapeutic support that profoundly altered my outcomes and life chances.

This is what remarkable and life-changing social work looks like. Quiet, often unrecognized, and yet profoundly important.

Early on, therefore, I came to terms with the fact that I might not be able to provide the support myself, but that I could undertake an assessment, collaborate with parents to help them see the benefit of change, refer to the appropriate support agencies and review the care plan. And ensure that all the support that could be made available was being made available.

My first manager supported me in developing these skills, and was especially keen for me to think about how we could improve the child's life, independent of what support and efforts were made to change the parent's behaviour. For example, I was encouraged to look at the role of extra-curricular or after-school activities to increase access to peers and safe adults, facilitate a sense of belonging, and support children in developing a skill, which might help their confidence and self-esteem. Another example would be collaborating with the school to think about what additional input they could provide, such as a homework club or additional Maths and English classes. Improving attainment can be crucial to improving outcomes for children and young people from disadvantaged backgrounds.

When reading *Working with Denied Child Abuse* (2006) by Andrew Turnell and Susie Essex, I came across an idea that helped me think about how we support children and families.

Copyright © Turnell & Essex in 'Working with Denied Child Abuse', Open University Press (2006). Used with permission.

The first way we can help a family is by identifying an issue and then seeking to help the parent with that particular issue. For example, if a parent has a drug or alcohol problem, we encourage them to think about change, and make a referral to the drug and alcohol service. We identify the risk, and then we encourage and support the parent to address the issue that has been construed as problematic for them and their children.

The second way, as we have just been exploring, is to identify support with the family system or through professional interventions that could ameliorate the impact of the issue on the child. The social worker who referred me to Young Carers did nothing to change my mum or dad, but she did refer me to a support group that significantly altered my experiences of growing up in my family.

Limitations of support services

In terms of identifying key issues and the type of support that was provided, this was relatively straightforward, formulaic even. If a parent had an issue with drugs and alcohol, I referred them to the drug and alcohol service. If the issue was domestic abuse, I directed the victim to the Freedom Programme and the perpetrator to a perpetrator programme. If the issue was mental health, the parent was asked to visit their local general practitioner (GP) to consider pharmacological remedies (i.e., medication) and to access some short-term talking therapy. Not infrequently, parents would be asked to do all three. Once I had made a referral to the relevant services, my job – as I saw it – was to review engagement with these support services and assess whether changes were made. A high premium was placed on engagement with services when I started because, well... how else would they change?

However, I encountered a few limitations with this approach. First, I wasn't specifying what the local authority needed to see to be satisfied that we didn't need to be involved – I was providing them with a list of services for each problem. When a parent had engaged in the service, as I had asked, and yet there was still an ongoing issue (the support didn't have the desired effect), I would find another type of support. Some parents complained that I was moving the goalposts or asking them to jump through hoops. This was frustrating for everyone.

I felt responsible for identifying the issues and finding the relevant support. When parents wouldn't make use of the identified support, I felt annoyed – annoyed that they weren't using the resource after I had gone to all that effort to make it available, but also annoyed (with myself) because I didn't have any other way to help them if they didn't engage in the support. I found myself having many dissatisfactory conversations about why they hadn't gone to their drug and alcohol appointment this week, or why they weren't at home to meet the family support worker.

Second, I found that many of the issues were more complex than the simple piecemeal pre-prescribed short-term services that were available for them. For example, I worked with many parents due to domestic abuse, but it couldn't be defined in the straightforward way I had been taught about at university, with the male as a controlling and coercive perpetrator and the female a victim. There were a few examples of this – for example, Peter and Alison.

But often, the domestic abuse was typified by what Emeritus Professor of Sociology at Pennsylvania State University, Michael Johnson, called 'situational couple violence' (2008). In situational couple violence, verbal and physical disputes arise due to living in poverty, disagreements on how to handle the children, drug and alcohol misuse and poor verbal skills. Dichotomizing the issue by sending the men on perpetrator programmes (or asking them to leave the home) and the women on victim programmes stigmatized the men and didn't help the couple find ways of managing conflict or dealing with the issues that were generating the conflict.

As another example, I have worked with parents who suffered from poor mental health, and I asked them to visit their GP, and the result was that they were often prescribed medication. Reviewing the parent's compliance with their medication then became part of my role, which was completely futile and seemed to make no difference as to whether they would take their medication regularly or not. I, myself, had also never managed to take more than two days' worth of a five-day prescription of antibiotics because I would forget. So I felt like a hypocrite asking them if they had taken their pill every day.

It also wasn't apparent to me whether using medication to resolve mental distress was especially effective. Several years later, I felt vindicated after reading Johann Hari's international bestseller, *Lost Connections: Why You're Depressed and How to Find Hope* (2018). He persuasively argued that the positive effects of taking antidepressants are minimal, and are often accompanied by plenty of adverse side effects. Hari points out that benefits might be worth it if suffering with significant distress or feeling suicidal (because at the extreme ends of mental distress, a tiny bit of help can go a long way). And that there are other benefits derived from speaking with a doctor and being provided with a story about mental distress. But on the whole, the effects are limited. So here I was, expending all this energy hypocritically asking a parent to take a medication that, on the whole, may have limited efficacy.[1]

Third, it didn't matter how severe the issue was – the type of support was often the same. Whether someone was suffering from a low-level cannabis problem or a 20-year heroin addiction, I would refer them both to the community drug and alcohol service, where they would access one-to-one support sessions once per week, and maybe a group. Whether a parent had mild depression or a chronic and severe borderline personality disorder, I would send them to their GP and for a six-week counselling course. Despite recognizing these issues, I could not see that there was an alternative way.

Learning from Turnell's Signs of Safety

This changed when I learned about Signs of Safety, a relationship-grounded, safety-organized approach to child protection, which I originally learned through a two-day course delivered by Viv Hogg at my local authority and then during a five-day residential course in the White Swan Hotel in Northumberland led by Andrew Turnell. Some key ideas revolutionized my approach to children and families and reinvigorated me when I was beginning to feel discouraged about the impact I was having.

Turnell flipped my perspective on helping families 180 degrees. I was focused on the problem and how it could be fixed. Turnell argued that our role was to describe the changes we needed to see, and then collaborate with the family on how that might be achieved. This was hugely liberating because I no longer felt the burden of identifying the support, and then felt unduly responsible for ensuring

---

[1]   I am not making any recommendations treating depression – that must be done by a qualified specialist. Medication can help people, especially when offered alongside other forms of treatment. Please see NICE guidelines, which offer evidence-based information: www.nice.org.uk/guidance/ng222/chapter/ Recommendations

engagement and change. Instead, I could focus on identifying what needed to change and enlist the family's help and partnership in finding a way to achieve that.

By focusing on what needed to change from a behavioural point of view, it was clearer to the parents what would need to happen before we could end our involvement. I could avoid the frustration experienced by parents when I gave unclear expectations. I became less focused on service provision and clearer on what needed to change. How they achieved those changes was up to them, and it didn't matter how they achieved it so long as they did.

This might include accessing the support I previously would have asked them to attend, but it might not. As pointed out by Turnell, in my signed copy (yes, I am that sad) of his *Safety Planning Workbook*:

> Child Protection professionals and courts tend to send parents and families to services, therapy, treatment, and educative services as a proxy for child safety. In reality, children are made safe through specific behaviours and actions taken by adults in their everyday interactions, most particularly at moments of difficulty and danger. (2013, pp.60–61)

For example, imagine a parent who binge-drinks alcohol. When I first qualified, I would have simply referred them to the community alcohol service and monitored their engagement. However, beginning with a vision of what needed to change, I could explain that 'for social care to no longer be involved, we need to see, over six months, that John is always in the presence of an adult who is not under the influence of drugs and/or alcohol'. Once this was established, I could ask the family how this could be achieved and how it would be monitored and reviewed. This approach, Turnell points out, requires skilful use of authority, honouring the parent's strengths, vision, conversation and compassion.

Any plan intended to improve safety in the life of the child must have rules that address the key concerns and particular stressors or triggers, such as:

HELPING CHILDREN AND FAMILIES 139

- How a couple will deal with conflict to avoid violence
- How a parent will deal with depression, anxiety or other mental distress and still ensure the children are taken care of
- How the parents will deal with their use of drugs and alcohol
- What will happen if the parent is struggling with any of the above issues, that is, can a family member be contacted to take the children out? What can the extended family do that might ease the impact of the issues on the children?

A central component underpinning the approach systematically outlined by Turnell is the role of the family network as a source of safety. I found, however, that parents would sometimes feel apprehensive about this, either because they didn't believe there was anything to be concerned about or because they felt embarrassed. This is understandable. Who would feel comfortable involving family, friends and loved ones to discuss a problem that you're experiencing, especially a personal one? It takes tremendous courage to open a dialogue with friends and family.

Often, parents will express relief afterwards because the experience lifts the burden of shame. They sometimes have more support than they realize. Hindsight, unfortunately, isn't available when they decide to agree to a family meeting. Following Turnell's training, I empathized with parents about their apprehensions, explaining to them that although this might be uncomfortable, it was one of the most effective ways to help them, and ultimately get social care off their back. I found this usually worked to overcome their fear. In families where our involvement is statutory, for example, child protection, pre-proceedings or in care proceedings, we can stipulate one minimum requirement: identify at least five people who can help and agree to attend a meeting. Of course, no one can compel them to do this. Therefore, they still need to be encouraged with tact and empathy for their position to maximize the probability that they will be willing to attend such a meeting. In my experience, it is very rare that parents will not want to do this.

However, the most important lesson I took from Turnell is not written in his books or in any of the vast Signs of Safety literature; it is, however, an underpinning feature of it all. In spending those five days training, learning from and observing him in Northumberland, I watched someone with a profound, if not sacred, spiritual commitment to honouring the individual. In the case of the training I attended, he directed this towards the child protection social workers, but it was easy to imagine how this would manifest in his work with parents. In advocating for a strengths-based approach in working with parents, he conveyed a tenacious and skilful commitment to discovering the pre-existing strengths of the child protection social workers in the room that was inspiring and left an indelible mark on me.

Re-thinking the role of support services

I faced two challenges in not relying on support services as the primary vehicle, however. First, when I had to issue care proceedings because change was not forthcoming and the risk to the children was unmanageable, I was heavily scrutinized for the support I had provided to the parents. Ensuring that every effort and support has been provided before permanent removal is considered is undoubtedly a sound and indispensable principle. However, on the witness stand in court, I found that I was generally cross-examined about the quantity of the support rather than the quality.

This had a downstream effect on practice because if I was ever sufficiently concerned to think that we might end up in care proceedings, then making all support available and having clear expectations about engagement with this support was necessary. Otherwise, I would be in court without much argument or chance of securing the relevant orders.

Second, there were some parents for whom support was absolutely necessary, but the available support seemed inadequate. In *Raising Parents* (2016), Crittenden outlines a framework called 'The Gradient of Interventions' that changed my thinking on support for parents.

The basic principle underpinning this is that the greater the parent's reflective capacity, the less intense the resource will need to be to help. Conversely, parents with limited reflective capacity will require more intense and significant support. For example, *parenting programmes* work best for parents with high levels of reflective capacity and need new techniques and ideas that they can apply in what is otherwise a relatively well-functioning household. This is a low-resource support service.

Short-term counselling is another low-resource support service, and in my experience, it is suited to parents with a single-issue adverse life event or for someone who understands their problems but needs another perspective to help them. I did not find this suited parents who had severe or enduring psychological and relational difficulties, which accounted for most of the parents I worked with.

Somewhere in the middle is *parent–child intervention*, for parents who recognize that they have difficulty in their relationship with their child and need help accurately perceiving their child's needs. In other words, they have some reflective capacity but require a relatively intense support service to help them improve their relationship with their child.

A parent with significant psychological or relational issues and low reflective functioning requires a resource-intense service such as *adult psychotherapy*. For a parent with an addiction, they will need support with that beforehand, and generally, the more severe the addiction, the more intense the treatment will need to be.

The most resource-intensive service is *adult life assistance*. There are some families where the level of need, psychologically and practically, is so great that they require ongoing services that help the family meet their children's needs. It might be that there isn't any intervention that will 'fix' the issues within the family, but with ongoing care and support, the children can remain safely in their parents' care.

When I think about my dad, who was abandoned by his mother, removed from his father, subject to multiple placements, and then had two decades' worth of addiction under his belt before he was ready to access support, I can see starkly the absurdity of expecting him to overcome his trauma, entrenched personality issues and addiction by attending six sessions of talking therapy with a trainee psychologist, or by accessing a community drug and alcohol service once a week. Yet this was what I found myself asking parents to do with not dissimilar backgrounds and issues.

My dad went to a residential rehabilitation centre where he accessed daily intensive psychological and relational treatment. Indeed, the research I have read suggests that residential treatment is the recommended option for individuals with severe and chronic addiction issues. Following this, he attended a secondary care unit before he was rehabilitated at home. Even once home, he continued to access Alcoholics Anonymous and the 12-step programme on a regular and consistent basis.

If he hadn't had access to this support, I am sure that he wouldn't have ever experienced sobriety in his adult life, and the outcomes for me would have been very different. Maybe I wouldn't have been writing this book. I might, however, have been sat in a residential treatment centre writing my life story, sharing the unbearable shame and guilt that I had put my children through what my dad had put me through, despite knowing full well how detrimental it would be.

I realize here that I am pointing to an issue about service provision for parents that most social workers don't have influence over. For that reason, I deliberated over whether to include it. But unless we recognize the inadequacy of the service provision, we limit our capacity to help children and families. Although I am not advocating for implementing support services that aren't already available, with leadership, vision, courage and persuasion, we could shift how we help parents, and make some of these more intensive, appropriate and effective forms of support available.

Conclusion

In this chapter, I have outlined several limitations of the relationship between a social worker and a parent. I didn't have time to offer parents practical help. Similarly, my ability to help therapeutically was constrained. What could I realistically hope to achieve visiting one hour a fortnight? Especially when you considered parents' experiences throughout their life, and the many much more significant, other influences on their life (critical relationships with family, partner and children, work and work colleagues, housing, community, etc.)? This doesn't mean that the relationship isn't essential, however. It is fundamental in at least three ways.

First, I must uphold the child's rights and manage these with the rights of the parents. When the child's right to protection supersedes the parent's right to private family life, I explain these processes transparently and humanely. Second, I can endeavour to collaborate with the parents, build on their strengths, establish shared goals and allow them to determine how they will achieve the goal of increasing child safety. And third, I can't make parents change, and nor can I force them to access support services. But I can have a conversation with them where they are provided the space to consider the possibility of change.

CHAPTER 8

Making Decisions and Removing Children

MATTHEW WAS A THREE-YEAR-OLD BOY with brown curly hair and large brown eyes. Matthew lived with his father, Steven, who was an alcoholic. Steven was drinking from morning to night, leaving Matthew to care for himself or with whoever he could get to look after him. The home was sparsely furnished, with few toys, and Matthew slept in a stained, often urine-soaked, cot. Occasionally, I would get angry reading about the lives that children had lived, and this case was one. I was angry at Steven. And I was angry that it took us so long to do anything.

Two years of constant neglect, punctuated by incidents such as Steven fighting with a neighbour, leaving Matthew with a 12-year-old family member and not returning for 18 hours, and Steven shoplifting, using Matthew and his buggy as a decoy. The extensive professional input made no difference, in part because Steven didn't believe he had a problem. He was frequently angry and blaming towards professionals; 'You lot make me drink I'm so stressed. Everything would be fine if you lot would just piss off out of our lives.'

We eventually ended up in court and Matthew was placed into foster care. He was filthy, with knotted, nit-infested hair, deeply embedded dirt beneath his nails, and wearing clothes that were far too small for him. He could barely speak and appeared withdrawn, disconnected and sad. Steven refused to provide me with any clothes or toys for Matthew to take with him: 'If you want to take him, don't

145

think I am helping you.' After this, Steven went off the radar and didn't see Matthew for several weeks.

Matthew flourished in foster care, and it was delightful to see his progress every time I visited him. He transformed into a bright and happy toddler, started talking and became much more mobile. Eventually, Steven began attending supervised contact and he began accessing treatment for his alcohol addiction. I started my parenting assessment of Steven.

He told me that his parents had taken very little interest in him, leaving him to bring himself up, 'There weren't around at all really, down the pub mostly or arguing with each other, I just looked after myself.' He said, 'School was shit, never had the right stuff, trainers and all that so just got my head kicked in all the time, which is basically what my dad did to me at home, probably my fault to be fair.' When asked whether he had any friends, he said 'I had one, Billie, did everything together but he moved when his parents separated. I was in Year 8, and I never saw him again.' He left school with few qualifications, 'I was thick as fuck, never understood what the teachers were saying, but felt proper embarrassed so I'd just kick off, then started not going…biggest regret, if I'm honest.' He secured a job at the local factory and met his first wife, Sophia, 'I thought we would be together forever, everything felt good when I was with her and we had a good life, well, better than I could of wanted.'

However, after he found out that Sophia was having an affair with one of their neighbours, he began drinking. Sophia ended the relationship and moved in with their neighbour while his alcohol use spiralled out of control. Depressed, addicted to alcohol and I suspect suffering with feelings of being worthless and unlovable, he felt his older children would be better off without him and he stopped seeing them, 'I just didn't see the point, I thought they'd be better without me, I was a shit dad to 'em.'

After several years, he eventually met Mandy, and within a few weeks Mandy was pregnant. Mandy had several physical health complications. She was also traumatized by sexual abuse in her childhood. She was happy to be pregnant, having believed that it wasn't possible due to her health. Tragically, she died soon after giving birth to Matthew.

Over the course of the assessment, Steven also began attending the drug and alcohol service, got sober, and even provided a clean hair strand drug test. He improved his home, tidying and decorating the place. He started attending contact consistently, and while his play with Matthew was very limited, he was well intentioned and took on board advice that he was given. However, on a few occasions during the latter stages of the assessment, he was observed drinking alcohol.

Faced with the option of Matthew remaining with his current carers – who absolutely adored him – with a plan for him to be adopted or return to live with his father, I concluded that the former would be in Matthew's best interests. I reasoned that while Steven had made significant progress, this was very recent, and he had lapsed on at least two occasions. Given the chronicity and severity of Steven's addiction to alcohol, I assessed the probability of a full relapse to be high, and if that happened, the care Matthew would experience would be dangerously neglectful. Matthew would need to be re-accommodated. He would experience further disruption, be placed with different foster carers, and would perhaps be too old to be adopted.

Adoption, on the other hand, seemed to present few risks. I agonized over this decision for weeks, losing sleep at night over it, and had several conversations with my manager to weigh up the options and clarify my thinking.

The Children's Guardian's report came in a few days later. I had a strong emotional reaction when I read the recommendation that Matthew return to his father's care. I felt sick. And then I felt angry. How could they not see what would happen to Matthew if he went home? Did they not care about Matthew? Had they read the chronology? Did they even know Matthew? How many times had they met him, once, twice? I barely slept that night.

Following legal advice at court, I resentfully conceded to the Children's Guardian's recommendation, and Matthew returned home to live with his father under a Supervision Order.

This was one of my first court cases where I had been confronted with one of the most complex decisions to make as a social worker: whether a child should stay and reunify with a parent, or be removed and placed into alternative care. I knew I was anxious about making the right decision, but I thought I had objectively analysed the options and arrived at an evidence-informed decision. My reaction revealed how emotionally invested I was in achieving a certain outcome when that outcome was suddenly taken away.

On reflection, there were a couple of reasons for this. I had spent several months being Matthew's social worker and had read a lot about his history through writing the chronology, reading several professional reports about his progress in different areas of his life, reading weekly foster care reports, writing looked after child reports, attending meetings and observing him in contact. I had become attached to him, and he really meant something to me. I wanted him to be happy, safe and well looked after. In my mind, weighing up the evidence and advocating for him to be adopted was an act of care – an act of love, even. So I felt gutted for him when I found out this wouldn't be an option for him.

Another reason, though, and one far less virtuous, was that I didn't like being wrong. The Children's Guardian disagreed with my recommendation, which was then ultimately approved by the courts, which essentially meant that I was wrong. A bitter pill to swallow.

There were a couple of important lessons from this experience, and similar experiences like it. It was not my job to decide Matthew's future. Thank goodness! That is an unbelievably complex decision for one person to make. My job was more modest, but no less serious. I had a responsibility to advocate for what I believed to be in Matthew's best interests and articulate those views using evidence, thoughtfulness and analysis, and with consideration of the different consequences. My role ended there.

It was ultimately the judge's decision; the judge was responsible for weighing up my evidence, the Children's Guardian's evidence, and the parents' evidence. There is a reason why these processes are in place. And over the years, I have come to appreciate this and recognize my place within them.

Although it took me a while, I eventually agreed with the Children's Guardian. My initial reaction was that I would need to be taken off the case because we would be pursuing a plan I fundamentally disagreed with. However, after a few emotionally tumultuous days, I realized that this was the plan the court endorsed. If this was what they decided was in Matthew's best interests, my job was to make sure that I did everything within my power to ensure it succeeded. Matthew was slowly reunified into his father's care, and I held regular family and professional meetings to review progress and areas for improvement. It was a bumpy path, but we ended our involvement with Steven and Matthew a year later.

The impact of separation

On reflection, I didn't fully consider the risks of Matthew being permanently removed in weighing up the decision. I underestimated the power and importance of Matthew's relationship with his only remaining parent. For Matthew, if the plan I recommended was enacted, he would need to transition from foster carers, with whom he had a close and affectionate relationship, to adoptive parents, whom he was unfamiliar with. This separation, no matter how well handled, would be almost as traumatic as separation from his father, as the adults whom he had come to trust and rely on would no longer be available to him.

At three years old, Matthew couldn't understand this properly. So the thoughts, feelings and sensations he experienced in response to a change in primary caregiver and the feelings of rejection and abandonment could be stored in his body. Unprocessed, embodied and unconscious trauma could make Matthew vulnerable as he grew older to reacting in irrational, self-destructive, yet self-protective ways in response to situations, events or sensory input that triggered an implicit memory of this past event. In other words, if there were relationships where he felt a tinge of rejection or experienced a felt sense of anticipated change, he might react *as if* he were responding to an actual rejection or abandonment.

To defend against those feelings, he might lash out at himself or in his relationship with others. He wouldn't know why he reacted this way, and when asked by others, his answer would likely baffle those around him. Consequently, they might even think he was being manipulative or doing it on purpose.

In addition, I hadn't considered that adoption wouldn't succeed. After subsequently working with adoption breakdown, I learned that adoption is far from the 'happy ever after' narrative I had naively believed. Although the rate of adoption breakdown is relatively low, especially for young children placed for adoption, a significant proportion experience significant challenges in adolescence.

Once adopted, even with safe and loving parents, children can often still yearn for their biological parents. Separation from biological parents often constitutes psychological trauma – a deep, primordial and often irresolvable despair that can scar children, impacting on them throughout life. The wound can be taken care of with exceptional alternative care, but it never disappears. However, many children don't receive exceptional alternative care, and so the scar often remains a constant source of anguish.

In my experience some children learn to cope with the desperate yearning by disconnecting themselves from the feelings because it's emotionally intolerable. Some children can be extremely angry with their substitute parents, which is a way of communicating their distress that is more emotionally tolerable than acknowledging their sadness and vulnerable need for parental attention, affection and acceptance. This is why it can be hard to appreciate how children who have been separated from their parents truly think and feel.

Finally, I didn't think enough about Matthew's long-term future. A few years later, I would come to appreciate the long-term consequences of my decisions after seeing how many children would reconnect with their parents as soon as they turned 16, if not before. This is another sign of how much these relationships mattered to them. I could protect Matthew from some harmful care, but what would that look like when he was 18, 30 or 60 years old?

Ethical dilemmas and uncertainty

I received a referral from the ambulance service: 'pt [patient] intentional overdose polypharmacy medications, pt has child who called ambulance and welcomed paramedics into home, pt treated on scene.'

Carrie was a 15-year-old girl. Carrie's mum, Chantelle, had severe mental health problems. Chantelle lived a reclusive life, getting through her day on a cocktail of medications and several energy drinks. The home was untidy, unclean and not looked after. Carrie wasn't supported to manage her personal hygiene, and there were few boundaries, meaning that Carrie was often out in the community with older children. Her behaviour at school was deteriorating, and she was on the precipice of being permanently excluded.

After two years of working with Chantelle under child protection and pre-proceedings, we had already decided that we were going to issue care proceedings. After receiving the information from the ambulance service, I went to visit Chantelle, and asked if she would agree for Carrie to be placed into foster care under Section 20 of the Children Act 1989. Chantelle answered the door, 'Not today', and went to close it.

'Wait', I said, 'please, can we just have a conversation?'

Chantelle held the door ajar as I continued, 'I know that you probably don't want to see anyone, and it sounds really like you've had a rough time, can we talk about that please?'

Chantelle opened the door, and we walked through the narrow corridor of her flat into the living room. Chantelle told her story, but it was difficult to follow, 'She started kicking off saying I am the worst mum in the world, calling me a bitch so I said don't expect me to be home later.'

I asked her what had started the argument, and she said, 'Carrie doesn't realize that I got the social on my back.'

'She doesn't realize you have the social on your back?', I paraphrased.

She said, 'Yeah, I just want her to come home but she doesn't want to so I said I will top myself then.'

Trying to make sense of the logic, I paraphrased again, 'She doesn't want to come home and you said you would kill yourself?' and then I asked, 'Can you tell me what happened from the beginning and walk me through, step by step?'

Chantelle, frustrated by my inability to understand, retorted, 'I just told you, she wanted to go out with mates after school and I told her she needed to come home first, that is what you are always saying, that I don't know where she is, and look what happened, she called me the worst mum in the world and I said well, if you think that, then I will top myself, and I wanted to show her I was serious.'

I empathized with Chantelle's frustration, recognizing the underlying intention of her behaviour. I explained that we had already agreed to issue care proceedings, and asked if she would agree for Carrie to be accommodated. She was resistant to the idea and thought it would show Carrie that she was giving up on her, and despite all their difficulties, that was the last thing she wanted.

We expedited our application to the courts, and a few days later secured an Interim Care Order. After the hearing, I returned to the family home, and when I told Carrie what was happening, she was upset but relatively calm. We drove together to the placement. When we arrived, I tried to ask the carer all the questions I thought a child in a new place might want to ask but feel too nervous to do so. In front of Carrie, I asked the foster carers, Laura and Michael, 'What happens if Carrie needs the toilet at night?', 'What are your rules about getting a drink?', 'If Carrie was feeling hungry, could she help herself, or do you like to be asked first?', 'What are the rules about phone use?', 'What do you tend to do in the evening?' and 'How would Carrie wake up in the morning? Do you wake her up?'

Initially, Carrie settled in very well with her new carers, their two children and the cat. A few months in, however, problems began to emerge. Carrie refused to go to school, and when she was in school she was getting into lots of trouble. Occasionally she would wake up in the middle of the night and leave her foster placement, meeting people she had met online in different parts of the country, and she wouldn't be found until several hours later. The relationship between Carrie, Laura and Michael was fantastic, but they weren't sure they could safely manage her late-night disappearances. A few days later, Laura and Michael provided 28 days' notice. My immediate reaction was not a positive or child-centred one.

'Bloody hell, I haven't got time for this.'

Then I felt angry towards Laura and Michael, 'What did they think they were signing up for when they agreed to look after Carrie?'

Then I reflected, 'Did I do enough to help Laura and Michael?' and 'What am I going to do now, because if Laura and Michael can't do this – when they have such a good relationship with Carrie – then who can?'

Eventually, my thoughts turned to Carrie, 'She has so much potential, but I am so worried that if I don't get the right placement, then we are going to make her life harder and worse, not better.'

After blaming the carers, then myself, before thinking about Carrie, I concluded with the following: 'I will do my damned best to find Carrie the right place so she can feel unconditionally loved and celebrated.'

At this point, I had to write the final evidence and care plan. I had to decide whether Carrie should remain in foster care or return to her mother's care. I knew that if she stayed in care, she would need to change placement, which would prove challenging to find and probably result in a change in school as it wouldn't be local. I also knew that for each placement breakdown, the risk of a breakdown in the subsequent placement increases as the child contends with further rejection and loss, which erodes away that capacity to trust.

Alternatively, Carrie could return home to Chantelle, where she would be severely neglected, exposed to her mother's poor mental health, probably end up permanently excluded, and spend increasing amounts of time in the community, increasing her risk of exploitation, antisocial behaviour and eventually, maybe, substance misuse.

Neither option held appeal; each was laden with risks, a recurring theme in the decisions I faced. Unlike scenarios with an evident superior choice over an obviously inferior one, I had to make a decision fraught with complexity. Although my purpose was to protect children from harm experienced in their parent's care, I found myself tasked with decisions that, regardless of the chosen path, promised harm – a harm that, rightly or wrongly, I would feel responsible for.

The weight of responsibility weighed heavily, knowing that Carrie's life outcomes would be significantly influenced depending on my decision. These instances, marked by the inevitability of distress, were some of the most emotionally challenging and anxious-ridden experiences in my career. Martin Hollis and David Howe captured this complexity in a paper called 'Moral risks in social work':

> Each case requires a decision, after due enquiry, whether to remove the child from home. Removal is a deeply disturbing, perhaps traumatic, event for all concerned and especially for the child. Failure to remove can mean the abuse of the child, or even its death. The choice is beset with powerful, usually opposed, emotional forces and prone to intense, usually unforgiving, public attention. (1987, p.123)

Harry Ferguson, in his book, *Child Protection Practice*, puts it like this: 'the fact that often there is no outcome that satisfies everyone and that some people should feel destroyed by what social workers have to do is a painful truth that is at the heart of the ethical complexity... in effectively performing child protection practice' (2011, p.150).

In the midst of trying to deal with the discomfort and enormity of the decisions I was expected to make, I came across an idea in Eileen Munro's book, *Effective Child Protection* (2008), called the decision tree. The decision tree didn't alleviate all my anxiety when making these types of decisions, but it did provide a systematic framework through which to make decisions. It made me feel more confident that I had carefully weighed all the options and possible consequences.

The decision tree is an antidote to deductive reasoning. An example of deductive reasoning would be the following sequence:

1. The child is at risk of harm in their parent's care, therefore
2. The child's safety could be secured by placing them in foster care.

Following this logic, any child suffering significant harm should be removed from their parent's care. However, it overlooks the harm of removal and any potential risks associated with being placed in alternative care, such as foster carers who don't connect with the child, or the child experiencing multiple placements. Munro advocates, therefore, for the decision tree, which has seven steps:

1. What is the decision to be made?
2. What options are there?
3. What information is needed to help make the choice?
4. What are the likely/possible consequences of each option?
5. How probable is each consequence?
6. What are the pros and cons of each consequence?
7. The final decision involves multiplying each probability score with a utility value and adding them together to reach a final score.

One benefit of this approach is that it encouraged me to consider more variables. For example, if I was deciding whether a child should be brought into foster care using the decision tree, I would outline the possible consequences of each option – remain at home or foster care.

If looking at foster care, the consequences could be:

- That the child has a very stable placement for the rest of their childhood
- They could have a mostly positive, stable placement and a possible breakdown (perhaps in adolescence), or

- They could experience very little stability with multiple placements.

An assessment would then need to be made about how likely each consequence would be.

When I looked into this, I was surprised by how few children had stable, lifelong placements. According to the Children's Commissioner's *Stability Index 2020*, the stability of placements among children in care over a three-year period was concerning: 47 per cent of children had one placement, while 53 per cent experienced one or more moves; specifically, 30 per cent had two or more placements, and 17 per cent had three or more. Additionally, more than 10 per cent of children who entered care experienced four or more placements. In other words, the likelihood of a young person experiencing placement stability – an important indicator of positive outcomes for children in care – is less than 50 per cent.

Other factors would need consideration. A child's age when they enter care can have an impact, with younger children more likely to achieve stability. The availability of high-quality placements can also make a difference. And so can whether the social work practice is proactive instead of reactive. How a child enters care makes a difference – for example, social workers who place children in care under an Emergency Protection Order don't have the time to find the best available placement, making sure it's the most suitable fit. There is no time for preparatory work.

When I secured Emergency Protection Orders in the past, I always felt an immediate sense of relief as I no longer had to worry about the children. However, the cost of ensuring short-term safety was often outweighed by the problems it caused, such as inappropriate matching with carers, organizing and supervising family contact and assessing the parents while the children didn't live at home. Part of the reason children who are adopted (compared to other forms of alternative care) achieve greater stability is that there is a much more extensive matching process.

Changing perspectives, changing thresholds

Over time, like many social workers who have been qualified for a few years, I became more appreciative of the limitations of alternative care. Sometimes it is necessary, and sometimes it requires us to passionately advocate and pursue that as an option. However, cultivating an awareness of the limitations meant that I was more willing to tolerate some of the risks that the child experienced in their family home, and work harder to try to help the parent.

This shift wasn't just child-centred; it was also about self-preservation. After spending years on one case, culminating in a five-day final hearing, the local authority was granted full care and placement orders. This was a case where there was no ambiguity that the children couldn't live with their parents. When the judge announced the final orders, I felt an overwhelming sense of relief. I felt proud of what I had secured for these children, content that they would be protected.

After years of trying to help the parents, I had spent the last few months fiercely advocating for the children to be removed due to the serious, pervasive and chronic level of harm they were experiencing. The nature of care proceedings is adversarial, and the effect is that I felt like I was in a fight, intellectually at least. By the time I walked out of the court and stepped into the lift, I felt sick to my stomach. It dawned on me how this was going to affect the parents. These parents, who had caused irreversible and severe harm, who had angrily resisted all support offered over the last two-and-a-half years, were victims of their social context and upbringing.

I never blamed them for their difficulties, but in trying to secure the right outcomes for their child, I had bracketed out some of their emotional reality and pain. Indeed, if I was too empathetic with them, I don't think I would have been able to bring myself to do what I needed to do to secure the outcome I felt their child needed and deserved. Now, however, empathy for their predicament washed over me, draining the life out of my body. I felt disgusted with myself for being part of a system that inflicted such unimaginable pain on another, and questioned the ethics of it all.

I stopped by the shop as I walked back to my car, bought a pack of four chocolate bars and ate all of them sat in my car, quietly, as the rain pattered down on the windscreen, conveniently shielding me from the outside world. The emotions of the last five days and the decision just made were overwhelming, and the sugar dump took the edge away.

Over the next few days, I could hold multiple perspectives more successfully without being swallowed in the competing emotions, and rationally make sense of what had happened. But that feeling was one I didn't wish to experience again, which further contributed to my desire and commitment to supporting children to remain at home. If a child did need to be accommodated, then I would want to know that everything, and I mean, *everything*, had been done to avoid that.

Reflections on working with foster carers

In the end, Carrie remained with her foster carers, Laura and Michael. My work with Laura and Michael involved listening to their frustrations about Carrie and her impact on their family, demonstrating empathy, and resisting judgement. Then, and only then, could we explore reframing the meaning they had attributed to Carrie's behaviour.

At some point early on I realized that once a child came into care, my job was to maximize the chance that the placement would succeed. And in the same way it was important to do everything to help a parent, it was also important to do everything to help the foster carer (or family member). Simply because they are paid doesn't preclude them from experiencing all the challenges and conflicted feelings associated with looking after a traumatized child.

I also realized that I needed to help humanize the child's parents, because the foster carer could easily develop skewed views about the parents based on what had been written in the report about them. Even when reports are accurately written, they don't do any justice to the character of an individual. Furthermore, some foster carers could develop an understandable anger towards the parents for the harm they had caused the child they were now caring for, and perhaps – hopefully – even loved. Facilitating relations between foster carers and parents was critical for helping the child adjust and accept the foster carers, but also to help the parents and foster carers.

Conclusion

In this chapter I have shared some ideas to support decision-making. Social workers make decisions all the time, and it isn't expedient, possible or even necessary to extensively consider each one.

However, when faced with consequential decisions, we should move decision-making out of the unconscious and into a more deliberate, thoughtful and conscious process. Munro's decision tree is one of the most effective tools for doing this, although this is time-consuming, and when under time constraints with too much work, there are strong pressures to avoid slowing down.

In my experience, though, the cost is small, especially in light of the human cost of making the wrong decision. Furthermore, once I had used the decision tree a couple of times, I realized I could integrate some of the concepts to improve my decision-making on a day-to-day basis.

CHAPTER 9

Managing Time and Making a Difference

IN THIS CHAPTER, I will share the time management techniques I learned and how I applied them in my role. I will also explore the limitation of any time management technique in a role that expects too much, and share how the demands of the role affected me personally.

Time management techniques

When I first qualified, I had one time management technique: writing a 'To do' list. One tip I received from my manager was to break down larger tasks into smaller tasks. For example, instead of 'Write parenting assessment', this could be broken down into 'Write background information', 'Write child's needs section', etc. Another tip my manager gave me was to cluster together specific tasks – so instead of working through the list chronologically, cluster together similar tasks. For example, if there were one or two referrals to other services for each case I was allocated, I could put them together and spend an hour specifically on them.

Writing a 'To do' list allowed me to see everything that needed to be done, although I often felt overwhelmed by the length of this and paralysed about where to start first. Everything seemed equally important and urgent. One of the most valuable ideas I came across was the four quadrants from the international bestseller, *The 7 Habits of Highly Effective People* by the American leadership expert Stephen Covey: '**Urgent and important**'; '**Not urgent but important**'; '**Urgent but not important**'; and '**Not urgent and not important**'.

I quickly found that a whole day, or sometimes a whole week, would pass where I hadn't been able to prioritize some of the important pieces of work because I was 'busy' with the 'Not urgent and not important' tasks, such as answering every phone call and responding to every email. Or reacting to every difficulty a family would present with me by immediately getting up off my office chair, darting out of the office, like some emergency service, and driving around to the home – only to find once I arrived that it wasn't as urgent as it had initially presented itself, and there wasn't much I could do anyway. Certainly not more than I could have done on the phone.

Using Covey's four quadrants, I began to take my long 'To do' list and divide the tasks into one of the four categories. At first, this proved challenging. I was trying to balance expectations from an electronic system with built-in deadlines and tasks that would turn red on the computer screen if they were overdue. It's hard to overstate how much the colour of the tasks in my LCS (Liquidlogic Children's System) tray affected my well-being.

In addition, I had tasks from my manager, from the families I worked with, and requests from professionals, as well as trying to do the work I thought was important, such as writing assessments and undertaking direct work with the children and their parents. Over time, however, I began to identify the tasks that seemed to make the biggest difference versus those that were less impactful.

The most essential tasks I found were spending time with children and families, undertaking chronologies, writing assessments and developing support plans. These were the elements of the role I would refuse to take any shortcuts on. As much as possible, I would diarize my calendar so that these activities were mainly in the 'Not urgent but important' (Quadrant 2), trying to avoid them ending up in the 'Urgent and important' category (Quadrant 1). This was an ongoing, unending struggle.

There was always some crisis, catapulting me against my will into the 'Urgent and important' camp (Quadrant 1), like a sudden and unexpected deterioration in a case, an injured child I needed to take to a medical examination, an emergency application, etc. Therefore, the 'Not urgent but important' camp isn't a place where I arrived, but a constant battle and one worth fighting for; I wanted to work on what mattered or could not be avoided.

As for 'Urgent, but not important' (Quadrant 3) and 'Not urgent and not important' (Quadrant 4) tasks, I had to learn to put these in their place, either by batching them together, or not doing them at all. The challenge was recognizing them for what they were because they had a seductive quality about them. 'Urgent matters are usually visible', Covey writes, 'they press on us; they insist on action. They're often popular with others... And often they are pleasant, easy, fun to do. But so often they are unimportant!' (2004, p.151).

As Covey points out, these are the tasks that are easy, quick and fun, and provided me with a little kick of motivation as I ticked them off my list. The biggest culprit for me was email. I loved emails. I loved receiving them, I loved being distracted from a boring or difficult report to read one, and I loved replying. They made me feel important and wanted. They were fulfilling to respond to, as if I had actioned some critical tasks. They made me 'feel' productive. I noticed a couple of things, though.

First, the more emails I sent, the more emails I received. Second, when I went on annual leave for a couple of weeks, I would return to hundreds of emails. That's how important I was! But at least 90 per cent weren't useful or were no longer relevant. Most were corporate messaging, information about a family that didn't require a response, or someone asking me for information (often emailing a day or two later to say they had found the information elsewhere). Few of them actually required a response.

Therefore, applying the batching method, I tried to block out half an hour at some point during the day to read and reply to all my emails. At other times, I didn't answer. I became notoriously bad at corresponding through email.

When you can't do everything

Sometimes I would finish work on a Friday after putting in 50 or 60 hours, and it would feel as though I had more work than I had begun with at the beginning of the week. I just couldn't do it all. I had to abandon all hope in the illusion of complete control and mastery of my workload.

So I made two adjustments. First, I picked what I would focus on and prioritize. If I couldn't do everything, I would have to make some hard decisions about what to prioritize. In other words, the option wasn't available to do everything I had to; rather, I had to choose wisely what I couldn't do, and learn to live with the consequences. This was how I became an unreliable email responder. When you can't do everything, some area or aspect of your practice has to suffer (and you also then have to deal with the negative feedback that comes with it).

There were other areas, too, such as my case note recording. A lot of case recording is unnecessary. At the beginning, I would record everything. A saying got banded around in my office: 'If it isn't recorded, it didn't happen'. Like every rule of thumb, if taken as an absolute, it becomes absurd. Therefore, if I did a visit and didn't record every aspect of the visit, I felt like the visit didn't count. I would write lengthy case notes that read like a transcript. I eventually learned to become comfortable with only recording the most relevant details. For example, if I spent 40 minutes with a child getting to know them, and we didn't talk about any of their worries, I wouldn't record the whole conversation. Instead, I would write, 'Spent 40 minutes getting to know Joey'.

Second, I changed the metric for evaluating a good week. At first, I would judge my week based on how much of my 'To do' list I had crossed off. However, the list would sometimes grow throughout the week quicker than I could cross off the tasks. So I tried to measure the success of my week not by how much my 'To do' list had shrunk, but by how productive I had been.

One of the ways I measured my productivity was how many hours of 'deep work' I had managed to do. 'Deep work' was an idea I learned from an American non-fiction author and Professor of Computer Science at Georgetown University, Cal Newport, in a book named after the concept (2016). A key idea in the book, deep work is to schedule every minute of a working day. This was one of the most helpful and practical ideas I implemented. Once I had written my 'To do' list and categorized it using Covey's four quadrants, I would schedule the week ahead.

After completing my 'To do' list and evaluating the different tasks by urgency and importance, I would block time for my week using my calendar, for example 8–10.30am: Write case conference report; 10.30–11am: Travel; 11am–12pm: Core group; 12–12.30pm: Travel, etc. The advantage of this approach was how I spent my time during the week based on what I had pre-determined as important rather than less demanding, more exciting tasks that popped up during the week.

Newport distinguishes between 'deep work' and 'shallow work'. Deep work is impactful but requires high-level concentration (report, chronology, etc.). Shallow work activities don't need much concentration and can be done efficiently (phone calls, emails, referral forms, etc.).

A critical element of deep work is working in a non-distracted and concentrated way. Newport argues that each time you get distracted, it can take several minutes after the distraction to re-emerge in the deep work task fully. I found, for example, that I could easily lose two hours I had put aside to write a conference report by answering the phone to a parent, responding to a couple of emails popping up in the bottom right-hand corner of my screen, chatting to a colleague, suddenly realizing I needed a cup of tea, and then the loo.

Each distraction may only take a minute or less, but it would take me several minutes or more before I was fully immersed in the activity again. I learned to turn off my emails, ask my admin to field any phone calls, and put my headphones on to block out all background noise and distractions. Of course, I still needed a cup of tea every hour or so, and the loo.

Although scheduling out my week was always derailed in some shape or form – an emergency, a crisis or a colleague desperately

The value of relationships

Although time management techniques were important, my relationship with my manager and colleagues was the most effective and sustaining factor in my role as a child protection social worker. No matter how busy I was, I would never miss a team meeting. And that wasn't because they were always a very productive use of my time – occasionally they were – but because I placed such a high premium on the value of being part of a team.

In child protection – and in life – you are only as successful as those around you. I was incredibly blessed with extraordinary managers; I dread to think about the type of social worker I would have ended up without them. My colleagues were also hugely influential. They taught me assessment writing, direct work, managing time, and, most importantly, wisdom and compassion.

As well as my social work colleagues, I relied heavily on admin workers – although their job title doesn't reflect the impact and responsibility they could have. Indeed, based on how tactfully and sensitively they handled some phone calls, they might as well have been social workers. I nurtured my relationship with them, clarifying how I could best use them, and frequently expressing gratitude to them for their support, sharing with them how their support was helping me to make a difference. This appreciation also extended to colleagues from other agencies, as I realized that one way to improve my ability to help a child was to strengthen relationships with other agencies, especially schools.

I would try to be as strengths-based with other professionals as I would with parents, expressing my sincere thanks when they provided me with information about a child, or when they allowed me to use a room for a core group meeting. I would explain to them how they were helping me to improve the outcomes for the child I was working with. For example, if I had to contact a school and ask them to speak to the class teacher about a child to find out about their attendance, attainment and general presentation, I explained that having this information was really useful to help gain a picture of the child and their needs, and to think about what support might make a positive difference. I would thank them for taking the time to speak to me, acknowledging how busy they were.

Cultivating these relationships meant that, when I needed to ask for something – for example, to visit the child urgently in school or to ask whether the school would be willing to fund some breakfast clubs – I was more likely to receive a favourable response. In other words, the relationship I made could influence my ability to leverage the school as a source of additional support for the child.

The personal and emotional cost

Writing a 'To do' list, dividing it into four quadrants, and then block-ing out my time for the week ahead was the most effective set of solutions I could find to handle the overwhelming work I had to do. Relationships provided the emotional and practical support that made it possible. Did these techniques and relationships stop me feeling overwhelmed? No. Like many social workers, I often worked long hours just to keep on top of everything.

I never took work home with me and I never worked on the weekends, which was perhaps my saving grace. I established that boundary early on – giving myself time to breathe on the weekend was a huge factor that allowed me to continue for as long as I did. However, working at the pace and intensity the role demanded, with the emotional challenges involved, was exhausting, and sometimes a punishing way to exist. At times, I felt alone, struggling with the work, and I believed that feeling overwhelmed was my fault. Here is an excerpt from my diary, which I wrote after I had been in my role for four years:

It's official I am struggling!! It's a difficult position to accept because it feels like I am admitting to not being good enough, fast enough, efficient enough. My team is dissipating around me. Tomorrow we will have a shared lunch for 4 people because they are all leaving at the same time. I just can't seem to cope with the sheer volume of work I am expected to do. I feel that I am unable to please anyone in this profession. The parents dislike me because of the inherent nature of my role particularly now I am experienced most of my cases are complex court or child protection. Other professionals aren't happy because I can never complete things as quickly as they would like me to or even respond to their emails and phone calls. I'm really struggling to comply with court timescales with regards to work being completed so receive emails from Children's Guardians. I struggle to see children enough to spend the quality time they need and deserve for my relationship to be meaningful and beneficial.

And then things would settle down again, and I would plough on through. However, this was frequently to the cost of my health, well-being and relationships.

Life admin became a massive inconvenience, like getting my car to the garage for an MOT or attending to my basic healthcare needs. I had toothache for months and did not feel I had time to book and attend a dentist appointment. So I endured the pain, masking it with painkillers until it became unbearable. I learned that arranging to see friends during the week was a recipe for breeding resentment in my relationships as, most times, I would end up cancelling at the eleventh hour.

My work also had an impact on my relationships with my close family. Indeed, for everything I have said about time management, one of the biggest contributions to my effectiveness and ability to do the job was the support I received at home.

Be the change

In my opinion, child protection social work is one of the most emotionally and intellectually demanding jobs. I think far too often social workers have too high caseloads and are placed under extraordinary pressure in a system that overwhelms, often preventing us from doing the work we would like to do, could do and know that the families need. My way of handling this was to accept the system for what it was.

I didn't choose the system or design it, and I did not have much influence over it. All I *could* control was the type of social worker I could be within that system, and that was what I focused on. I realize this might sound fatalistic, but I found that focusing on issues over which I had no control or influence depleted my energy.[1] I wonder if my attitude here was influenced by a prayer I learned through attending AA meetings with my dad as a child, a prayer that is often on the walls in AA and said by everyone in communion at the end of each meeting:

> God, grant me the serenity to accept the things I cannot change
> The courage to change the things I can
> And the wisdom to know the difference.

Therefore, I tried to be the type of social worker I wanted to be, despite the working conditions. I tried to 'be the change' and:

- Demonstrate patience and kindness to a colleague asking for assistance when feeling overwhelmed
- Show compassion to a parent screaming personal insults at me
- Put aside my anxiety about my workload when seeing a child
- Build meaningful relationships in a system that made that very difficult.

Of course, these – somewhat – highfalutin' ideas and principles I aspired to didn't stop me from constantly complaining with my peers – that was our second favourite coping strategy, after humour!

---

[1] This isn't to say that I agree with the working conditions for social workers. I think far too often they are overworked, which affects them and their families. In my opinion, this is one of the main drivers behind the retention crisis currently being experienced in social work.

Conclusion

Child protection is hard. And it demands the very best of us. Learning time management techniques helped a lot, but I would be lying if I said that it removed the almost constant state of anxiety I experienced, either from feeling like I had too much to do or by being asked to do something difficult.

I think the context to undertake this role is harder than ever, and sadly, I don't envisage this changing dramatically anytime soon. Children and families, in the meantime, need and deserve social workers who are compassionate, thoughtful and resilient.

I have worked with some exceptional social workers, and I like to think that if you're reading a book on the topic, such as this one, you are one of them.

You get to define what constitutes the social work system. Each and every time you show gentleness to a child, intellectual rigour in an assessment, compassion towards a parent harming themselves or others, gratitude to your colleague – at that moment, at that very small moment – you are defining what constitutes child protection social work.

You are social work.

CHAPTER 10

The Child Protection Social Worker Role

IN THIS BOOK, I have shared what I have learned about some of the critical aspects of social work. I have also written about what the job entails, and how this has required me to adjust my understanding of the role. In other words, the job I ended up doing wasn't what I had been told or had read the job was about.

I will now try to answer the question directly about what the role of the child protection social worker is based on my experiences. To begin with, I will share what I think the job is not. Here are some common myths that I myself have held at some point, and I have discussed them throughout the book. I will briefly recap here, though, before outlining a definition of what I believe child protection social work to be.

What child protection social work is not
Myth 1

The first myth is that the role of a child protection social worker is to keep children safe and happy. This is how many social workers introduce themselves to children. Keeping children safe and happy is a worthy and desirable goal; however, this isn't possible for even children in the most privileged circumstances. Most children are endangered at some point. Indeed, a child who isn't allowed to take age-appropriate risks, to fall over and hurt themselves, is likely to grow up disturbed by their lack of autonomy and intrusive parenting that parents believe is required to keep them safe.

The goal of child protection work is to protect children from undue harm, which is much more modest and achievable. In other words, a child protection social worker can never eradicate risk. Instead, a child protection social worker can work with a family to reduce the risks to the child sufficiently enough to remove the need for statutory social work.

Myth 2

The second myth is that it is the job of child protection social work to make parents change. But we can't make people change. For some reason, it took me a long time – and many frustrating conversations – to realize this.

A moment of self-reflection may have prevented this painfully slow realization if I had thought about how difficult it is to get myself to change. This doesn't mean we can't help people change, and there are ways of having conversations that can increase the chances of someone's motivation changing. However, even with the use of particular communication techniques, the degree to which change can be brought about is dependent on the other person.

We can explain to parents what will happen and within what timescale should change not occur. We tell them about the possible consequences and, depending on their responses, determine which option is taken. This is closely related to the idea that social workers can function as quasi-therapists to bring about this change.

The challenge in attempting to provide such therapy is twofold. First, many parents fear social work involvement or don't believe they have a problem – and you can't offer therapy to someone who hasn't asked for it or accepted that they have a problem. Second, as a child protection social worker, I never had time. Even when children are subject to a child protection plan, social workers visit parents once a fortnight at most.

While there might be telephone contact and core group meetings, the statutory visit provides the best opportunity for building a relationship. During a statutory visit, social workers must share any recent concerns with the parents (some will accept, and some will object, minimize or deny, causing friction), check the home conditions and the bedrooms, and speak to the children.

A social worker typically spends 20–30 minutes per fortnight with a parent. That is the amount of time a social worker has to influence someone's thinking, way of dealing with feelings, patterns of behaviour, addiction and relationships.

Twenty minutes every fortnight adds up to 40 minutes per month, which amounts to 8 hours per year.

Eight hours out of a total of 8760 hours in a year. In percentage terms, 0.1 per cent.

In other words, 99.9 per cent of the time a parent is influenced by other relationships, life circumstances and factors. You could double, triple or even quadruple a social worker's time with a family – and the overall effect remains very small.

Other factors in a parent's life that are likely to be more impactful include their childhood and current relationships, such as with their children, parents, siblings, neighbours or a partner. They might have ongoing issues stemming from the past or current context, such as substance misuse or mental health difficulties. Or they might have financial issues, housing problems, health issues, employment problems, etc.

Myth 3

The third myth is that it is our role to help children and families. Helping families can be a byproduct of our legislative role of protecting children from harm, but it isn't always the case that we help families. Or at least, it isn't apparent we 'help' when we use the word in the conventional sense.

When I have been involved in a child being removed from their parents, it cannot be said that I am 'helping'. All the parents I have worked with find the removal of their child extremely distressing and traumatizing, and children are also usually traumatized by it. Nevertheless, it might be the necessary action to ensure the child's safety.

If I measured success based on whether I 'helped' a family, then, in many instances, I would feel like a catastrophic failure. Instead, there needs to be a different way to think of the role of child protection social work, one that is less based on the outcome and more focused on the process. Forrester (2017) likens the social work role to one of a judge because a judge isn't evaluated on the outcome of a court case, but instead on whether they handled the case fairly. For example, did the judge use the law judicially, respect the suspect, review the available evidence with rigour, and show balance? And so that is also what should be an outcome to aspire to in child protection social work – the way we treat children and parents, and whether we have applied the law with proportionality, and maximized the chance of the parents being able to make the necessary changes.

So what is child protection social work then?

Now for the hard part. If it is not those things, what is child protection social work? I offer two key ideas: upholding rights and ethics.

Upholding rights

I think child protection social work, at a fundamental level, is about upholding rights (Forrester 2024). Our society has decided to allow parents to bring up their children in any way they choose – unless, of course, their parenting results in their child suffering harm. However, we must balance the child's right to protection with the parents' right to a private family life. When children are harmed, the social worker needs to decide whether to uphold the parents' right to a private family life or to prioritize the child's right to protection. Such a decision has to be underpinned by key principles, such as including the perspective of the child and their parent. Not uncommonly, the parents might have expressed a wish for social work not to be involved.

A key question that social workers commonly face is, 'Should I impose statutory involvement in pursuit of the child against their wishes, or uphold the parents' right to a private family life?' Sometimes this is straightforward, for example, when the child is at extremely high risk and the parents are unwilling to accept statutory involvement. Other times, it is marred with complexity where there is some evidence that the child has been harmed, ambiguity about the impact of harm on the child, yet legitimate concern that failure to intervene will result in the child being further harmed.

The complexity of this dilemma is only intensified when a decision has to be made about whether a child can remain safely at home or needs to be placed into alternative care. The law is that children should be protected from significant harm, and raised with their family of origin; however, it also states that if the child suffers significant harm, then alternative care might need to be sought. Again, the issue is of competing rights. Ideally, if children are removed from their parents' care, they would be placed with a family or friend. If not, they are afforded stability in an alternative arrangement, such as foster care and adoption.

Suppose a child is removed from their parents' care. In that case, the parent and child's right to ongoing contact with one another must be respected, and both should be involved in key decisions affecting their lives. Again, these have the potential to create tension. As Professor Jill Duerr Berrick from UC Berkeley explains in her book, *The Impossible Narrative: Navigating the Competing Principles of Child Protection*, 'Children should have a say in a decision that affects their lives but what if what they want hurts them? Children should be safe. But what if their safety is compromised when they live with their family? These are not merely philosophical debates; child welfare workers live out these conflicts on a daily basis and must regularly favour one principle at the expense of another' (2018, p.6).

Therefore, most frontline child protection social work is consumed by handling these competing rights and dealing with everything required in between. For example, although we want children to be protected from harm, we realize that the best way to achieve this is by helping the parents change or providing support to offset the risks. Therefore, in pursuit of this endeavour, it makes sense that we form partnerships with the parents and try to collaborate on how this can be achieved. Learning how to work with parents, some of whom don't want to work with social workers, therefore becomes a critical element of our work.

In the previous eight chapters I have shared some of the lessons I have acquired in upholding rights. Fundamentally, though, I believe rights are achieved through proactive case management. While it is undoubtedly essential to build relationships, we must also learn to convene meetings, review plans, advocate for children and families for resources, build effective relationships with other professionals, write referral forms, write assessments and understand research on various topics, such as domestic abuse, substance misuse, etc.

For example, if after years of working with a family to bring about change unsuccessfully, and the harm experienced by the child is such that I think alternative care is required, it is not my relationship that will make the difference. Instead, it will be how well I can put together an evidentially robust, child-centred, balanced and thoughtful parenting assessment that can withstand the scrutiny of the courts. Of course, the degree to which I can write this assessment will be underpinned by the quality of my work with the family.

Can I demonstrate:

- I have done everything within my power to support the family, including identifying support from professionals, family and the community?
- I have been transparent with the parents about the key concerns and given them a chance to respond?
- Evidentially, the child has suffered significant harm that is attributable to the parents' care of them?
- I have understood and integrated the parent and the child's wishes and feelings into my analysis?
- I have weighed up the effect of separation on the child and family?

Ethics

I think child protection social work is about ethics. In particular, we need to develop our own personal and professional ethics. I am not referring to the Code of Ethics prescribed by organizations such as the British Association of Social Workers (BASW), Social Work England (SWE) and the International Federation of Social Workers (IFSW). Although they all have important things to say, I don't find them especially helpful with 'on-the-ground' ethical challenges.

Essentially, it is about asking ourselves, 'What type of social worker do I want to be?' and developing principles to uphold, irrespective of the conditions. What type of social worker would you want knocking on your door if you were traumatized, exhausted, struggling with addiction or in a violent relationship? How would you like a social worker to treat you if you reacted with fear, anger or avoidance?

A central ethical principle for me is the relationship. Although I have mostly downplayed the role a social worker can play in the life of a child and their parents, I still believe that the relationship is essential in at least two ways. First, I want children and parents to feel that I care about them deeply and personally. Even though I have to make decisions they might not agree with, or have difficult conversations with them, I still want to convey a profound, almost sacred, regard for their humanity. Second, I want to treat children and parents with respect and dignity, irrespective of how they treat me.

I have many other ethical principles, but the idea I am advocating for here is that each social worker establishes their own ethics and values so that they mean something. I think these two central ideas – upholding rights and ethics – make child protection an invaluable role in society and one that is interesting, emotionally challenging, and intellectually taxing. This work is 'imperative', as Professor Jill Duerr Berrick writes:

> The safety of children is at stake. But their work is extremely challenging. Each child has any variety of special needs and circumstances, and many families present with multiple, complex issues.

As they work to secure children's safety, caseworkers must earn children's and parents' faith that they share a common interest in the well-being of the child – this, against a backdrop of high emotional intensity, anger, and fear. They wield the enormous power of the state with the authority to recommend the ultimate devastation to a parent: the removal of a child from a parent's home. But child welfare workers rarely feel like powerful actors. Constrained by limited agency resources, sometimes overlooked by judges or attorneys whose professional titles wield greater status, and too often targeted in the media when mistakes are made, child welfare workers carry out difficult work. (2018, p.2)

If we want to live in a society whereby children are protected from harm, yet with caution and respect for the parent's right to a private family life, then we need social workers to undertake this extremely challenging task.

Imagine what our society would be like if children were left to be severely and chronically neglected or abused by their parents or family. Or if social workers could readily and permanently remove children from their parents' care without evidencing and justifying the decision. Neither of these would make for a good society. Therefore, social workers are tasked with this unbelievably crucial societal goal of navigating between these tensions.

And in pursuit of this noble and worthwhile goal, I think there is an opportunity for us as social workers to define how this work is undertaken. In our small way, each of us gets to determine what constitutes the child protection system, and in the process, learn and grow ourselves.

Personal reflections on the role

As I draw this book to an end, I am mindful to acknowledge that we have experienced a climate of political instability as well as deep and extensive cuts to many services that support vulnerable children and adults. It is a testing time. There are many government initiatives intended to improve children's services. Sometimes they bring about positive changes, and sometimes they make little difference. There is always an evolving landscape of knowledge, theory and policy that is difficult to keep abreast of.

Despite this changing and uncertain landscape, I believe some unchanging elements exist in our role as child protection social workers. Since the inception of child protection in the late 19th and early 20th century, social workers have needed to build relationships with parents, connect with the children to understand their lives, and find ways to offer help (Ferguson 2004) – and when necessary, decide to secure children's safety by placing them with others. That is what I have focused on in this book. I have no grand theories or approaches to revolutionize the system, and some might point this out as a limitation of the ideas I have advocated for in the book.

I believe frontline case-holding social work is one of the most important jobs in our society. It is incredibly challenging, and not everyone is cut out for it; indeed, only a few of those drawn into it stay in it for a prolonged time. It is emotionally, physically, intellectually and relationally demanding. It is fraught with moral challenges and ethical dilemmas.

Few jobs expect you to spend the morning writing a 30-page report deciding on whether a child should be removed from their parent's care, and then spend your lunchtime visiting a traumatized and distressed child in a school, before heading to court to be cross-examined and heavily scrutinized for the past 18 months of your work with a family. Or where one moment a mother is cuddling you, thanking you for the help you have given her family, and the next moment another parent is calling you a 'fucking cunt'.

I'm amazed that anyone does it, ever.

And I am in awe of anyone who takes on that role, and even more impressed by anyone who does it for a sustained period. Doing the job takes tremendous courage, tenacity and grit. It requires wisdom, professional maturity and humility for what can be achieved. Other traits, such as patience, compassion and reflexivity, are also needed.

We must take our role seriously, handling it with the utmost care, yet not take ourselves too seriously. Sometimes social work is framed in moral and idealistic ways, such that you would be led to believe that the social work profession has a monopoly over virtue. I don't always recognize the social work in these descriptions – partly because many other professions have similar values, but also because my practice was messy and fraught with anxiety, self-doubt and uncertainty.

There was no comforting illusion of providing a neat and packaged intervention that would transform a parent's life, and thus their child's life. The parents I worked with faced unimaginable adversity that was rooted in systemic oppression and intergenerational patterns of harm – people weren't so susceptible to change that I could turn their life around by showing up for six months once a fortnight, while also dealing with dozens of other parents with similar issues.

Some parents could not overcome the lifetime of trauma to provide safe care for their children; some were able to avoid the excesses of self-destructive behaviours such that it was unsatisfactory but good enough; and occasionally, just occasionally, some parents did change and indeed turn their life around by giving up a lifetime of drug addiction, leaving a violent partner or getting help for their poor mental health.

In all instances, when I ended my work with a family, their life went on. Some who didn't change when I worked with them would go on to turn their life around, whereas others relapsed, and almost all of them continued to face hardships. The effect I had on all families was unclear. I was a small piece among a wide range of variables and networks in the life of a family. In some ways, I was unimportant; in other ways, who I was and how I showed up was profoundly important. Life-changing, even.

If I allow myself to be sentimental, I will say that, at best, my intention that a child or a parent I was working with felt warmth and was unconditionally accepted would pierce through my professional aloofness and personal shortcomings. In these moments, where a connection was established despite my foibles and uneven power dynamics, I experienced a profound sense of purpose and affirmation in the value, importance and sacredness of the work.

Conclusion

In this book I have focused on what we, as individual social workers, can do and achieve. In my experience, success is found in small ways that often go unnoticed and unrecognized:

- When I managed to react with sensitivity (instead of fear and agitation) to an angry parent
- When a sentence I had written perfectly captured a child's experience in a report
- When I had a laugh with a young person while playing a game of FIFA
- When I chaired a child in need meeting successfully
- Or when a colleague asked a question regarding the electronic system that I knew the answer to.

In the midst of all the challenges within the role, these moments of connection, developing efficacy and helping others are what kept me going.

Mia, a small 11-year-old, had recently been removed from her parent's care and placed into foster care. She had just attended supervised family time with her dad and grandparents, who had left, and we were in the car park waiting for her foster carers to arrive. Standing by my car, Mia swung open the car door and scrambled onto the roof. She looked at me mischievously, waiting for my response. I couldn't help but smile at her tiny act of rebellion, especially when she began dancing. Encouraged by the spark of playfulness, I leaned into the car and cranked up the music. Heartened by her cheeky demeanour, I joined in, dancing in the middle of the children's centre car park on that warm, sunny afternoon – her on the roof and me down below.

In the words of Roald Dahl's *Matilda the Musical*, 'sometimes you have to be a little bit naughty'. And in that moment, with the sun casting a warm glow on our spontaneous dance, it felt like we were embracing the joy of mischief, experiencing a glimmer of light amid life's challenges.

That interaction won't be found in any report or assessment, recorded on a child's file in an electronic system or noticed by any inspector. I hope it will be found, however, in Mia's heart. As you will definitely find it in mine.

References

Baim, C. and Morrison, T. (2011) *Attachment-Based Practice with Adults: Understanding Strategies and Promoting Positive Change*. Hove: Pavilion Publishing and Media Ltd.

Black, A. (2020) 'Why we don't talk to children?' Richard Devine's Blog, 8 May. https://richarddevinesocialwork.com/2020/05/08/why-we-dont-talk-to-children

Burnham, J. (2018) 'Relational Reflexivity: A Tool for Socially Constructing Therapeutic Relationships.' In C. Flaskas, B. Mason and A. Perlesz (eds) *The Space Between: Context, and Process in the Therapeutic Relationship* (Chapter One). London: Routledge.

Children's Commissioner (2020) *Stability Index 2020: Technical Report*. 11 November. www.childrenscommissioner.gov.uk/resource/stability-index-2020

Covey, S.R. (2004) *The 7 Habits of Highly Effective People: Restoring the Character Ethic* (Rev. edn). New York: Free Press.

Crittenden, P.M. (1993) 'An information-processing perspective on the behavior of neglectful parents.' *Criminal Justice and Behavior 20*, 1, 27–48. https://doi.org/10.1177/0093854893020001004

Crittenden, P.M. (2008) *Raising Parents: Attachment, Parenting and Child Safety*. Cullompton: Willan.

Crittenden, P.M. (2016) *Raising Parents: Attachment, Representation and Treatment* (2nd edn). Abingdon: Routledge.

Crittenden, P.M. and Landini, A. (2011) *Assessing Adult Attachment: A Dynamic-Maturational Approach to Discourse Analysis*. London: W.W. Norton & Company.

de Montigny, G.A.J. (1995) *Social Working: An Ethnography of Front-Line Practice*. Toronto, ON: University of Toronto Press.

Department of Health, Cox, A. and Bentovim, A. (2000) *The Family Assessment Pack of Questionnaires and Scales*. London: The Stationery Office.

Dingwall, R., Eekelaar, J. and Murray, T. (1995) *The Protection of Children* (2nd edn). Aldershot: Avebury.

Duerr Berrick, J. (2018) *The Impossible Imperative: Navigating the Competing Principles of Child Protection*. Oxford: Oxford University Press.

Eagleman, D. (2011) *Incognito: The Secret Lives of the Brain*. Edinburgh: Canongate Books.

Featherstone, B., White, S. and Morris, K. (2014) *Re-imagining Child Protection; Towards Humane Social Work with Families*. Bristol: Policy Press.

Ferguson, H. (2004) *Protecting Children in Time: Child Abuse, Child Protection and the Consequences of Modernity*. Basingstoke: Palgrave Macmillan.

Ferguson, H. (2011) *Child Protection Practice*. Basingstoke: Palgrave.

Ferguson, H. (2017) 'How children become invisible in child protection work: Findings from research into day-to-day social work practice.' *The British Journal of Social Work 47*, 4, 1007–1023. https://doi.org/10.1093/bjsw/bcw065

Forrester, D. (2017) 'Outcomes in children's social care.' *Journal of Children's Services 12*, 2–3, 144–157. doi: 10.1108/JCS-08-2017-0036.

Forrester, D. (2022) Interview with Kayleigh Llewellyn, 3 February. Exchange Wales. www.youtube.com/watch?v=OAhfrV4qFf8

Forrester, D. (2024) *The Enlightened Social Worker: An Introduction to Rights-Focused Practice*. Bristol: Policy Press.

Forrester, D., Kershaw, S., Moss, H. and Hughes, L. (2007) 'Communication skills in child protection: How do social workers talk to parents?' *Child & Family Social Work 13*, 1, 41–51. https://doi.org/10.1111/j.1365-2206.2007.00513.x

Forrester, D., Westlake, D., Killian, M., Antonopoulou, V., *et al.* (2019) 'What is the relationship between worker skills and outcomes for children and families in children and families social work?' *The British Journal of Social Work 50*, 3, 883–905. https://doi.org/10.1093/bjsw/bcy126

Forrester, D., Wilkins, D. and Whittaker, C. (2021) *Motivational Interviewing for Working with Children and Families: A Practical Guide for Early Intervention and Child Protection*. London: Jessica Kingsley Publishers.

Hale, B. (2019) '30 years of the Children Act 1989.' Scarman Lecture 2019, Law Commission, London, 13 November. www.supremecourt.uk/docs/speech-191113.pdf

Hari, J. (2018) *Lost Connections: Why You're Depressed and How to Find Hope*. London: Bloomsbury.

Hollis, M. and Howe, D. (1987) 'Moral risks in social work.' *Journal of Applied Philosophy 4*, 2, 123–133. https://doi.org/10.1111/j.1468-5930.1987.tb00211.x

Horney, K. (1945) *Our Inner Conflicts: A Constructive Theory of Neurosis*. London: W.W. Norton & Company.

Johnson, M.P. (2008) *A Typology of Domestic Violence: Intimate Terrorism, Violent Resistance, and Situational Couple Violence*. Hanover and London: University Press of New England.

Kahneman, D. (2011) *Thinking, Fast and Slow*. London: Penguin.

Landa, S. and Duschinsky, R. (2013) 'Crittenden's dynamic-maturational model of attachment and adaptation.' *Review of General Psychology 17*, 3, 326–338. https://doi.org/10.1037/a0032102

Lewis, M. (2011) *Memoirs of an Addicted Brain: A Neuroscientist Examines His Former Life on Drugs*. Toronto, ON: Doubleday Canada.

Maté, G. (2018) *In the Realm of Hungry Ghosts: Close Encounters with Addiction*. London: Vermilion.

Ministry of Justice (2022) *Achieving Best Evidence in Criminal Proceedings: Guidance on Interviewing Victims and Witnesses, and Guidance on Using Special Measures*. January. https://assets.publishing.service.gov.uk/government/uploads/system/uploads/attachment_data/file/1164429/achieving-best-evidence-criminal-proceedings-2023.pdf

Munro, E. (2008) *Effective Child Protection* (2nd edn). Los Angeles, CA: SAGE Publications.

Munro, E. (2019) *Effective Child Protection* (3rd edn). Los Angeles, CA: SAGE Publications.

Newport, C. (2016) *Deep Work: Rules for Focused Success in a Distracted World*. New York: Grand Central Publishing.

Pennebaker, J.W. and Smyth, J.M. (2016) *Opening Up by Writing It Down: How Expressive Writing Improves Health and Eases Emotional Pain*. New York: Guilford Press.

Perry, B. and Szalavitz, M. (2017) *The Boy Who Was Raised as a Dog: And Other Stories from a Child Psychiatrist's Notebook: What Traumatized Children Can Teach Us about Loss, Love, and Healing* (3rd edn). New York: Basic Books.

Pinker, S. (2018) *Enlightenment Now: The Case for Reason, Science, Humanism, and Progress*. New York: Viking.

Porges, W.S. (2017) *The Pocket Guide to The Polyvagal Theory: The Transformative Power of Feeling Safe*. New York: W.W. Norton & Company.

Siegel, D.J. (1999) *The Developing Mind: How Relationships and the Brain Interact to Shape Who We Are*. New York: Guilford Press.

Skinner, B.F. (1953) *Science and Human Behavior*. New York: Macmillan.

Thomas, I. (2018) 'The gift of desperation.' TEDx Talk. www.ted.com/talks/ian_thomas_ian_thomas_the_gift_of_desperation

Turnell, A. (2013) *Safety Planning Workbook*. Perth: Resolutions Consultancy Pty Ltd.

Turnell, A. and Edwards, S. (1999) *Signs of Safety: A Solution and Safety Oriented Approach to Child Protection Casework*. London: W.W. Norton & Company.

Turnell, A. and Essex, S. (2006) *Working with Denied Child Abuse: The Resolutions Approach*. Milton Keynes: Open University Press.

van der Kolk, B.A. (2014) *The Body Keeps the Score: Brain, Mind, and Body in the Healing of Trauma*. London: Penguin Books.

Weick, A. (2000) 'Hidden voices.' *Social Work 45*, 5, 395–402. doi: 10.1093/sw/45.5.395.

Wolfs, R. (2008) *Adoption Conversations: How, When and What to Tell*. London: British Association for Adoption and Fostering (BAAF).

Index

ABC+D model 38
'Achieving Best Evidence'
    (ABE) guidance 58
*Adoption Conversations: How, When
    and What to Tell* (Wolfs) 65
Adult Attachment Interview
    72, 76, 77, 122
adult life assistance 141
Ainsworth, M. 38
Assessing Adult Attachment
    (Crittenden & Landini) 26
*Assessment of Children in Need and
    Their Families* (Department
    of Health) 107
assessments
    assessing change 125–6
    biases in 110–11
    case study 99–100
    components of 106
    identifying underlying issues
        121–5
    of parenting 102–6
    reasons for writing 100–2
    risk of harm 106–21
Attachment-Based Practice with
    Adults (Baim & Morrison) 44
attachment theory
and children 37–47

Baim, C. 36, 44
behaviour, patterns of 113–17
Black, A. 50
Body Keeps the Score, The
    (van der Kolk) 51

Bowlby, J. 38
*Boy Who Was Raised as a Dog,
    The* (Perry & Szalavitz) 33
brain development 33–5
Burnham, J. 52–3

case management 131–4
child protection principles
    change and consequences 95–6
    finding common ground 92–3
    good outcomes 93–4
    multiple perspectives
    valuing parents 91–2
child protection social work
    ethics in 177–8
    helping children and families
        173–4
    keeping children safe and
        happy 171–2
    parental change 172–3
    reflections on role 178–81
    upholding rights 174–6
children, removing
    case study 145–9
    changing perspectives over 157–8
    ethical dilemmas over 151–6
    and foster carers 158–9
    separation impact 149–51
    uncertainty over 151–6
children, working with
    and attachment theory 37–47
    brain development in 33–5
    case study 31–3
    and memory 36–7

children, working directly with
challenges of 59–62
difficult conversations 52–3
helping to understand
experiences 62–5
introductions with children 55–7
overcoming fears 51–2
practice with 54–5
protecting childhood innocence
50–1
purpose of 53–4
trust building 51–2
types of direct working 49–50
visit structures 58–9
Children Act (1989) 82, 151
Children's Commissioner 156
confirmation bias 110
conflict management 81–6
Connexions 21
Core Assessment 106–9
Covey, S. 161–2, 163
Crittenden, P. 20, 26, 27, 38,
41, 76, 78, 96, 140

de Montigny, G. 9–10, 11
deep work 164–5
Department of Health 106, 107
Developing Mind, The (Siegel) 36
Devine, Richard
empathy with parents 27–8
motivations to become
social worker 24–5
personal and emotional costs
167–8
practice in social work 25–7
redemptive healing and
helping in family 17–24
difficult conversations with
children 52–3
Dingwall, R. 111
drug and alcohol addictions 74–6, 89
Duerr Berrick, J. 175
Duschinsky, R. 38
dynamic-maturational model of
attachment and adaptation
(DMM) 20, 27, 38, 39, 41, 47

Eagleman, D. 37
Edwards, S. 92

Effective Child Protection
(Munro) 109, 115, 154
Essex, S. 50, 62, 86
ethics
in child protection social work
177–8
of removing children 151–6

fears, overcoming 51–2
Featherstone, B. 125
Ferguson, H. 10, 52, 81
Forrester, D. 55–6, 81, 96, 174
foster carers 158–9

Hale, B. 82
halo effect 111
Hari, J. 136
harm, assessment of
child's experiences of harm 119–20
and Core Assessment 106–9
Eileen Munro's ideas on 109–11
identifying family strengths 120–1
and past support 118
and social care involvement 112–13
understanding patterns of
behaviour 113–17
helping children and families
case management for 131–4
case study 129–30
and child protection social
work 173–4
effective helping 130–1
and Signs of Safety 137–40
support service limitations 135–7
support service roles 140–2
Hogg, Viv 137
Hollis, M. 154
Horney, K. 26
Howe, D. 154

Impossible Narrative, The: Navigating
the Competing Principles of Child
Protection (Duerr Berrick) 175
In the Realm of Hungry
Ghosts (Maté) 22
In My Skin (TV drama) 55
Incognito: The Secret Lives of
the Brain (Eagleton) 37
introductions with children 55–7

Johnson, M.P. 136

Kahneman, D. 111

Landa, S. 38
Landini, A. 26
Leigh, Sarah 23
Lewis, M. 89
Llewellyn, Kayleigh 55–6
Lost Connections: Why You're Depressed and How to Find Hope (Hari) 136

Main, Mary 38
Maté, G. 22, 75, 93
Memoirs of an Addicted Brain (Lewis) 89
memory in children 36–7
Ministry of Justice 58
Morris, K. 125
Morrison, T. 36, 44
Motivational Interviewing for Working with Children and Families (Forrester, Wilkins & Whittaker) 96
Munro, E. 109, 110, 115, 116, 154

neglect by parents 76–8
neurosequential model of therapeutics 35
Newport, C. 165
NICE 139

Our Inner Conflicts (Horney) 26

parenting assessments 102–6
parenting programmes 141
parents, working with
    drug and alcohol addictions 74–6
    case study 67–74
    neglect by parents 76–8
    symptoms and causes 76
parents, working directly with
    child protection principles 91–6
    conflict management 81–6
    psychological denial 87–91
    situational denial 86–7
Pennebaker, J.W. 51

Perry, B. 22, 33, 35
Pinker, S. 39
Porges, W.S. 59
protecting childhood innocence 50–1
Protection of Children, The (Dingwall) 111
psychological denial 87–91

Raising Parents (Crittenden) 38, 140
Re-imagining Child Protection (Featherstone, White & Morris) 125
Realm of Hungry Ghosts, The (Maté) 75
relationships, importance of 166–7

Safety Planning Workbook (Turnell) 138
7 Habits of Highly Effective People, The (Covey) 161–2
short-term counselling 141
Siegel, D. 36
Signs of Safety 50, 92, 130, 137–40
Signs of Safety (Turnell & Edwards) 92
situational denial 86–7
Skinner, B.F. 27
Smyth, J.M. 51
Stability Index 2020 (Children's Commissioner) 156
substance abuse 74–6, 89
support services
    limitations of 135–7
    rethinking roles of 140–2
Szalavitz, Z. 33, 35

Thinking Fast and Slow (Kahneman) 111
Thomas, I. 89
time management
    prioritizing in 164–6
    techniques for 161–3
    and workload 167–9
trust building 51–2
Tucker, Rob 56
Turnell, A. 50, 62, 86, 92, 137, 138, 139–40

van der Kolk, B. 18, 51
visit structures 58–9

Weick, A. 9
What You See Is All There Is
(WYSIATI) bias 111
White, S. 125
Whittaker, C. 96

Wilkins, D. 96
Wolfs, R. 65
'Words and Pictures' explanation 62–3
Working with Denied Child Abuse
(Turnell & Essex) 50, 62